To my father, Ray Jamiolkowski, and my uncles, Terry, Richard, and Edward Jamiolkowski, and Jim Hendricks.

Each of them helped to teach me how a father can sustain a caring, loving relationship with his family.

ABOUT THE AUTHOR ◇

aymond M. Jamiolkowski holds a bachelor's degree in elementary education and a master's degree in guidance and counseling from Northern
Illinois University, DeKalb. He undertook further graduate
studies at the University of Florida, Gainesville. Ray
taught grades two, five, and six at Edwin Aldrin Elementary School, Schaumburg. Illinois, and was an elementary school guidance counselor and testing and research
specialist for the Marion County Schools in Ocala, Florida.
He is the author of *Coping in a Dysfunctional Family.*

Currently Ray is serving his tenth year as a middle
school guidance counselor at Lincoln Junior High School,
Naperville, Illinois. Ray lives in Naperville with his wife,
Mel, his daughter, Jenny, and his son, David.

Contents

CHAPTER 1

What Is a Father?

Todd

Todd thought, "At least now there will be less fighting."

It was his way of consoling himself when his parents told him that they were planning to divorce. He wasn't surprised. The screaming and yelling; the door-slamming and leaving; the harsh words to him and the subsequent apologies all let Todd know that his parents would eventually divorce.

Todd's problem now became: Where will he live? Both parents think that, at fourteen, Todd is old enough to decide. Both have told Todd that he is welcome. Since his father has already taken an apartment in another town, Todd will not be able to alternate between homes during the week. He'll either have to stay with his mother and continue at his current school, or go with his father and change schools.

Todd sees advantages and problems in both plans. Changing schools might not be a bad idea. During the worst of the fighting, Todd's schoolwork fell off quite a bit. He was having trouble concentrating. But even when his grades dropped, no one seemed to care. A fresh start at a new school might be a good idea.

Todd has a good relationship with his mother. She is a good listener and helps him to sort things out. The problem with living with Mom is that she is planning to get a job and go back to college. She'll hardly ever be home, and Todd doesn't want to strain her already extremely tight budget.

Todd's father has a good job and a comfortable income. He works regular hours and seldom travels. But after fourteen years of living together, Todd feels that he doesn't really know him. His father has always been a good provider, but Todd doesn't know what he likes, what he believes, how he feels about things, or what's important to him. Todd just doesn't feel comfortable talking to him. He wonders if he could become closer to his father if he lived with him.

Nadine

Nadine has a collection of dolls from all over the world. Since she was very young, whenever her father went on a business trip he brought her back a doll from the country or region he had visited. When Nadine was young she loved the dolls. She played with them endlessly, imaging big families of children of all different colors living together happily.

When she turned twelve Nadine decided to store away some of her older dolls and display just a few of her favorites. She felt she was too old to be playing with dolls, but she wanted to keep them for her own daughter someday. Nadine wanted to tell her father that she was no longer interested in dolls, but he was so seldom home.

When he did come home from a trip with a new doll, she would appear ungrateful if she told him how she felt.

Now that she is fifteen, it makes Nadine a little angry that her father still brings her dolls. She would much rather he would take the time to get to know her, to find out who she is and what she likes. Each new doll creates a little more distance between them. Each doll makes her feel more alone.

Robert

Robert had never before had trouble in school, and his dean knew it. The other boy had pushed him, challenged him, and threatened him. Finally when the other boy hit him, Robert hit back. He hit back so hard that he may have broken the boy's nose.

The dean was sympathetic with Robert, knowing that the other boy had a reputation for making trouble, but Robert had gone too far by injuring him. The dean asked Robert, "Would it be better for me to call your mother or your father?"

Robert said immediately, "Please, call my mother!"

After placing the call, Robert and the dean waited. To pass the time, the dean asked, "Why did you insist that I call your mother instead of your father?"

Robert thought a moment before answering. He spoke slowly, "I really don't know why I said that. My father could have come over just as easily, I guess. It's just that I can explain things easier to my mother. She'll listen and try to understand my side. My father always sees things his own way.

"Don't get me wrong. My dad is a good father. I just don't feel close to him. He doesn't really know me or understand me. Maybe my mother can help me explain what happened to him."

HOW FATHERS RELATE TO TEENAGE CHILDREN

Parents today are trying to raise their teenage children in a society that is very different from the one in which they grew up. Different types of families are being formed. Men and women relate to each other differently. The interaction of mothers and fathers with their children is different from twenty or thirty years ago.

Changing Families in the Nineties

Once a typical family consisted of two parents and their two to four children. This typical family often drew its support from an **extended family** of grandparents, aunts, uncles, and cousins living nearby.

Today more than half of all marriages end in divorce. Single parents, stepparents, half siblings, stepsiblings, blended families, and shared custody of children are all very common. Families are often spread across the country, with members providing little support for one another. The fast pace of society, the constant change, and frequent moves to new towns make it difficult for family members to stay in close communication.

Male and Female Roles

Once the roles played by men and women were clearly—although many people would say unfairly—defined. Men were expected to find a career and provide financially for a wife and a family. The woman's role was to care for the children and the home. For generations men and women followed these roles.

The past thirty years have seen a complete breakdown of these roles. Women have achieved equal opportunity for jobs. They are encouraged to pursue a satisfying career. A large number of mothers work outside of the home. The role of financial provider is no longer strictly a male role; likewise the role of caring for the children is not primarily a female role.

Mother and Father Roles

Laws are now in place allowing women to accept their opportunities in the workplace. A short maternity leave after childbirth, followed by a return to work and subsequent child care is a common pattern in young families today.

At the same time, society has been slow to change the role of fathers. Men who grew up expecting to provide for a family are now called on to help raise, nurture, and care for their children. The majority of fathers are raising their children in a family that is very different from the one in which they grew up. They have few guidelines or role models and little experience.

Children and teenagers need their fathers more than ever before. In the past, fathers were needed for protection and financial security. Now they are needed for caring, understanding, and emotional support. Movements have arisen in the country to help men to develop the skills to bridge the emotional distance between father and child. In the meantime, many teenagers need help in coping with their father.

As important as fathers are to their teenagers, roadblocks may make it difficult for children to relate to them:

abandonment, living away from home, imprisonment, homosexuality, physical disabilities, addiction, divorce, previous abuse, and difficult situations in their own upbringing. Each of these can make emotional closeness more difficult. Often the roadblock cannot be removed, but teenagers can learn to cope with it.

STRIVING FOR EMOTIONAL CLOSENESS

In any emotionally difficult situation, people need strategies. Coping is best achieved by understanding the situation thoroughly, challenging ourselves to change those things that can and should be changed, and accepting those things that cannot be changed.

Coping Comes from Understanding

People cope best when they know and accept the truth. Pretending or imagining never really helps in the long run. Some teenagers imagine that their drug-addicted father will stop any day now. Some teenagers whose father is in prison pretend that he is there because he did something important or noble. These notions are called **denial**. Typically, denial is an immediate reaction to a tragic situation. For a short time, denial can help a person get through a situation that is too painful to accept initially.

In the long run, the truth must be faced and accepted. Drug addicts rarely change without professional help. People in prison are there because they broke the law. To cope with a father who has made serious mistakes, it is essential to face the truth.

Try to change only things that *can* be changed. It is frustrating to try to change another person. Few people can clearly see how someone else should change for their own benefit. It is even more difficult when that person is your own father, who has seen you change and grow from an infant to a teenager.

Sometimes teenagers can improve their relationship with their father by changing their own behavior. Being more patient, being a better listener, slowing down, and trying to see your father's point of view may all help to bring you closer together.

It is important and healthy, however, for a person to be himself. Changing your behavior to become closer to your father does not mean pretending to be someone that you really aren't. The goal is for you and your father to communicate: clearly, regularly, and honestly. Playing a role or pretending to be someone else to please your father is dishonest.

Accept Things That Cannot Be Changed

Divorce, physical disability, abandonment, and imprisonment all are paternal conditions that teenagers will not be able to change. Expending time, energy, and emotion on situations that are not changeable is wasteful. Coping usually means living with and accepting things that you find uncomfortable, unpleasant, or undesirable. Trying to change things that cannot be changed leads to frustration for you and for your father.

CHAPTER ◇ 2

Emotional Distance

The changes in families over recent years have tended to make family members drift apart. There are numerous reasons for fathers' emotional distance from their children. Among them, society's expectations have changed. Fathers are trying to raise children in a family very different from the one in which they grew up. Work keeps fathers away from home for extended periods of time. And unfortunately, many fathers are having difficulty coping with their own challenges but have not yet learned to seek and accept help for themselves.

SOCIETY'S CHANGING EXPECTATIONS OF MEN

At one time men knew precisely what was expected of them in our society. As women gained equal rights and equal access in the workplace, however, the distinctions between women's and men's roles blurred. Women are now taking an important role in providing financial resources, whereas men are expected to take a larger role in raising their children.

We are at a time when many mixed messages are being given on television and in the movies. Men are depicted as being incapable of fulfilling a parental role. On some shows the plot revolves about Dad's being unable to change a diaper, feed a baby, or perform simple household chores. These situations suggest that society expects men to take a parenting role but they depict the men as not yet able to assume that role.

It is frustrating for fathers to try to meet expectations when they are unclear as to what the expectations are. Both parents in a two-parent family need to work out their areas of responsibility in a fair way. When both parents are contributing financially, both are also responsible for contributing to the emotional well-being of the children.

LACK OF A CURRENT ROLE MODEL

Meeting parenting expectations is difficult for many fathers because the family they are attempting to raise is very different from the one in which they grew up. If a man had a cold and distant father, it is hard for him to develop a warm and close relationship with his own children. If his father left all the parenting to the mother, he may have trouble fairly sharing the parenting with his wife.

All of these difficulties can be overcome. It may take time, patience, and understanding by each family member to allow everyone in the family to feel close, safe, and secure. Sometimes reading books, talking to other fathers, or sharing activities with other families can help fathers to expand their parenting role. In other cases, individual, group, or family counseling is necessary to break down the emotional barriers.

Travel for work, a long commute to work, divorce, and separation all create physical distance between fathers and their children. These barriers make it more difficult for them to be close emotionally. If the quantity of time that a father can spend with his family is limited, the quality of the time must be improved.

THE FATHER'S OWN CHALLENGES

Fathers suffering from addiction, substance abuse, legal difficulties, or poor self-esteem find it difficult to meet the emotional needs of their children. Their best recourse is to seek help for their own problem. It is easy for a child to resent a parent who is self-destructive and who has no plans to change. On the other hand, it is important to forgive and try to forget when a father is making a sincere effort to recover from his disabilities.

If a father is addicted to alcohol, drugs, gambling, or any other compulsive activity, it is important that a child not accept or encourage his addictive behavior. Sometimes children make excuses, lie, or cover up for a father in the belief that they are protecting him. In truth, they are simply enabling him to continue his addiction. Such a pattern of making life easier for an addict or alcoholic is called **codependency**.

Communication Goes Two Ways

It is possible remain close if both father and child make a sincere effort to listen, wait patiently, and try to see the other's point of view. If neither of you is trying to become close, you must take the first step. In that way you may actually encourage him to listen more patiently and understand you. Sometimes you must state your needs directly:

"Dad, I need to talk to you."
"When can I talk to you about——."
"Can I ride with you to the store? There's something I want to talk to you about."

Finding the Right Time

An important part of communication is timing. If you are talking when no one is listening, or listening when no one is talking, no communication is taking place. You need to be observant and determine whether this is a "good time" to talk.

Sometimes you simply need to ask for time or schedule a time to talk. Asking your father when you can talk is a reasonable and mature first step toward becoming closer.

Patience and Persistence

Finally, changes in relationships between people take time and patience. When a father or child sincerely wants to become closer emotionally, it may be necessary to wait until the other person is ready. This may require many small steps, many long conversations, or simply a long time.

Don't give up. If you and your father are emotionally distant, it may take a very long time to improve your relationship. But if you are able to bridge the emotional distance, you will both have a satisfying and fulfilling relationship for the rest of your lives.

CHAPTER ◇ 3

Fathers and

Daughters

Carla

Carla Ruggio was going to the Homecoming Dance with Mike Shapiro. This would be Carla's first formal dance, her first date with Mike, and the first time she had gone out with a guy old enough to drive. As you would expect, Carla was nervous and excited.

Mrs. Ruggio had taken Carla to several shopping malls to pick out a dress. They disagreed frequently about colors, styles, and price. Carla was often critical of her mother's taste in clothing. As their shopping progressed, Mrs. Ruggio gave in a little on style but held firm on the amount of money she was willing to spend. Finally, after about a dozen stores, mother and daughter found a dress on which both could agree. Carla apologized for being so fussy. She told her mother that she didn't mean to be difficult; she just wanted everything to be perfect.

Carla's feelings about the dance went up and down. Half the time she was a nervous wreck, fearing that she would say or do something embarrassing; the other half she was giddy with excitement. Mrs. Ruggio was used to Carla's ever-changing moods. When Carla was grumpy, Mom would either measure her words carefully or try to joke Carla out of her mood. When Carla was excited, Mom helped to keep things in perspective. Carla and her mother disagreed on a wide variety of subjects, but they both accepted the fact that disagreements happen. When either one crossed an invisible line and went too far with her comments, she apologized to the other. Not surprisingly, it was Carla who most often overstepped the boundary. She appreciated the fact that Mom understood.

Carla and her mother got home just as Mr. Ruggio returned from one of his frequent business trips. He greeted them both with a smile and asked where they had been. Carla told her father that they had bought her a dress for the Homecoming Dance. Mr. Ruggio responded, "That's nice, dear."

There was a part of Carla that wanted her father to be at least a little more interested in her life. She didn't expect him to take a great interest in the dress itself, but he could at least have asked when the dance was and with whom she was going. But she concluded that he was tired from the long plane trip; they would talk about the dance later.

After dinner Carla was in her room, where she could distinctly hear conversations in the family room—a fact unknown to her parents. Carla's mother was explaining to Mr. Ruggio, "While we were at the mall, Carla and I spent some of our time shopping separately. I bought this gold necklace for her. I think it would mean a lot to her if you gave it to her to wear to the dance."

Mr. Ruggio replied, "Fine."

Carla was hurt. She didn't expect her father to take much interest in the dance or, for that matter, in any part of her life. But now she was angry about her parents' deception. How many other gifts had her father given her over the years that were really gifts from her mother? Did her father think about her at all?

The day of the dance was filled with preparations and appointments. The hairdresser alone took two and a half hours. Carla was far too busy to think about her feelings about her father, her mother, or even about her date. Everything was hectic, but it seemed to be going great.

About a half hour before it was time to leave, Mr. Ruggio knocked on Carla's door. He walked in and handed her the beautiful gold necklace. He looked deep into Carla's eyes and said, "I knew that this would go perfectly with your dress."

Tears filled Carla's eyes. She realized that her father had never even seen her dress before. How could he know that the necklace went with it? Even now he hadn't commented on how she looked. It really would have boosted her confidence for him to tell her that she looked good. She felt deceived, cheated by the gift that her mother had bought for him to give.

Mistaking Carla's tears for tears of joy, Mr. Ruggio smiled warmly at his daughter and closed the door on his way out.

HOW FATHERS AFFECT
THEIR DAUGHTERS

Emotionally, Mr. Ruggio has never been close to Carla. He provides an income for his family. Each member is safe and healthy. But Mr. Ruggio depends on his wife to provide for Carla's emotional needs. Mrs. Ruggio has become so accustomed to her husband's emotional neglect that she covers up for him. On an important day in Carla's life, she has done everything a mother could do to support her daughter. She bought the necklace thinking that by giving it to Carla her husband would seem to be doing his part as well.

Carla had already accepted the fact that she was closer to her mother than to her father. She didn't expect him to take the same interest as her mother, but she was disappointed that he hadn't taken any interest at all. It seemed as if Carla was being raised by a single parent.

FATHERS ARE ROLE MODELS FOR THEIR DAUGHTERS

It is not uncommon for fathers to leave many of the parenting chores to the mother. Fathers are often heavily invested in their career. They see their role as making money and the mother's as raising the children. Actually studies have shown that a daughter's relationship to her father is extremely important in guiding her to develop the kinds of relationships she will need in her own family one day. Girls learn about becoming a wife and a mother from both of their parents. Very often young women choose to develop relationships with men who are either very much like their own father or dramatically different from him. To be emotionally healthy, a person needs to be connected emotionally to other people who are significant in their lives. Girls learn about developing these relationships by observing their own parents, but more important, by developing a healthy connection with each of them.

Many fathers have never experienced an emotional connection with their own father. These fathers don't connect emotionally with their own children, because they don't know that they're supposed to. They often need to be told directly what their daughter needs. What Carla needed was not a gold necklace, but her father's time, interest, and attention. Mrs. Ruggio could have helped him give a much greater gift if she had made him aware of Carla's real wishes.

HOW DAUGHTERS CAN BECOME CLOSER TO DAD

To cope with any difficult, unpleasant, or unhealthy situation, a person needs to ask a few questions. Some questions will help, and others will only make the situation worse. When coping with an emotionally distant father, it is important to draw the line between your problem and your father's problem. Trying to make an emotional connection with your father by yourself will not generally work. On the contrary, it will most likely make you more bitter and angry than ever. It is important to recognize that parents have an obligation to meet their children's emotional needs.

Questions That Will Make the Situation Worse

What did I do wrong? Is this my fault? How can I change to make my father want to be closer to me? Why doesn't my mother straighten this out?

These questions remove the responsibility from your father. They will do nothing to help him recognize his obligation to meet your needs. Girls often believe that they could have been better daughters, that they weren't sweet, patient, or good-humored enough. They take the blame for their distance from their father. This kind of thinking fails to recognize that adolescence and childhood are a time of learning. Much of our learning comes from making mistakes and receiving correction. We would never know about those invisible social lines that separate acceptable and unacceptable behavior unless someone let us know when we crossed them. Parents need to tell children when they have gone too far. Maturity is reached, not by avoiding mistakes, but by learning from the mistakes that we do make.

Questions That Can Help

Can I do anything that would help my father to change? How can I cope if change is impossible?

Sometimes it is possible for a daughter to help her father to change. A first step might be to talk it over with someone you trust who is already close to your father. For Carla, her mother would be a logical choice. She could use her mother as a sounding board to figure out ways to help her and her father to connect. Other girls might talk to an aunt, an uncle, their grandparents, or a neighbor who knows their father well.

The next step is to communicate your feelings clearly. Explain to your father that you would like to become closer to him. Don't bring in how neglected you feel, what a great relationship other girls have with their dads, how close you are to your mother, or how poor a father you think he has been so far. Such comments may actually serve to push you farther apart. You need to begin by finding common ground.

You might open the conversation by asking him:

"How are things going at work?"

"Do you remember that town we stopped in when we went on vacation last year?"

"Could you help me with my jump shot?"

"What did you think about that story in the paper this morning?"

Once you open a conversation, it is important to listen. A key to communication is to understand the other person before you explain your point of view. If you take time to try to understand your father's perspective, it will be much easier to convey your ideas to him in terms that he can understand and accept.

Another step is to be patient. You may have a great, deep, important talk with your father, followed by days or weeks of disconnection. Now you need to go back to find the common ground that helped bring you together. Don't be surprised if it takes a while for your communication to improve. As a teenager, you probably have adjusted to a fast-changing world, whereas your father may be more comfortable with routine. Changing the ways that you communicate and hear each other may be unsettling for both of you at first.

Some fathers strongly resist change. If you have patiently and persistently tried to become closer to your father without success, try to appreciate the close adult relationships that you do enjoy with your mother or other adults. You may already feel close to an uncle, an aunt, your grandparents, or a neighbor. Try to listen to and share your feelings with them. No one can take the place of your father, and no one should. But other adults can help you to understand yourself and your role someday in a caring relationship with another person.

If your father is completely unable to bridge the

emotional distance between you, try to appreciate him for who he is. Understand that a warm house, food, and living expenses may be all that he is able to give you.

CHAPTER ◇ 4

Fathers and Sons

Mark

Murray Brooks thought of himself as a good father. He earned a decent salary as sales manager for a car dealership. He was able to provide a comfortable home for his wife and two sons. He was also setting money aside for the boys' college funds. Unlike some men he knew, Murray was home every night. He didn't gamble, drink excessively, or fool around with women. Murray told himself that he was always there for his family.

Lately the car business hadn't been very good, however. Even the people who still had jobs were watching their money carefully. Murray tried reducing prices, increasing advertising, and even laying off some of his newer salespeople. But none of these moves helped profits.

Recently Murray had been experiencing some shortness of breath, and his heartbeat seemed to race at times. He didn't mention these symptoms to anyone. He had good health insurance, but he was afraid that if he spent any time away from work the whole place would go under.

Each evening before he opened the front door, Murray paused and put on a big smile. "How's everyone today? Work was great. Those new cars are something else; we can't keep 'em on the floor. What's for dinner? I'm famished."

His wife smiled and thought, "Same old Murray."

Both boys reflected, "Same old Dad."

Things were not going well for Murray's son Mark. Mark had just started his freshman year at a parochial high school. The school had a strong reputation for preparing students for college. It also had a winning tradition on the football field. Mark was not excelling in either area.

His courses were harder than he had expected. He worked long and hard but was getting Ds in algebra and history. He was failing biology. Every minute of every day was dedicated either to homework or football.

Football wasn't going too well, either. Mark was seldom on the field for scrimmages. Although he made it through all the cuts, it was clear that he was one of the last ones kept. By now, Mark figured that the only reason that the coach wanted him around was to embarrass and humiliate him. He rode Mark harder than anyone on the team, yet he never put him into a game.

Frustrated and miserable, Mark went to his school counselor. The counselor listened and said, "It sounds as if you are overextended. Some students have a hard time balancing academics and athletics. Have you talked to your parents about dropping football?"

Mark said he hadn't, but that he would. The problem was that he usually talked things like this over with his mother. She was a good listener and was able to help him sort out the issues for himself. However, Mark's mother was out of town helping her sister with a new baby. Mark would have to talk to his father.

When Murray came home, it was all smiles as usual. "Hey, with your mother away, how about the three of us go out for pizza."

John said, "I can't. Play rehearsal tonight. I ate already."

So Murray looked at Mark. "Well, it looks like you and me."

They ordered a deep-dish pizza, and the waitress said that it would take about thirty-five minutes. "Good," Mark thought, "I can talk to Dad about football and school."

Murray started talking about baseball, the new car lines, a trip he took to Florida as a kid, and a variety of other subjects. Mark was having a tough time breaking in. Finally he said, "Dad, I need to talk to you about school."

"That school! I'm so proud of your going to a school like that. You'll get a scholarship to whatever college you want. Both athletic *and* academic." Murray went on for minutes about what a great school Mark was attending.

Mark tried another approach: "Actually, Dad, I wanted to talk to you about football."

This brought on fifteen minutes of memories about Murray's high school football career. "If it wasn't for that knee injury, I would have played in college, too."

Mark decided that he would just wait until his mother got home. They ate their pizza and talked about professional basketball. At the end of the evening Murray let down his guard a little bit: "I really enjoyed this. We should talk more often."

Murray smiled to himself. He was proud of his sons. He was proud of himself. When he was growing up he was never comfortable talking to his own father. Murray Brooks was sure that he was raising his boys right.

WHAT SONS LEARN FROM THEIR FATHER

The kind of adult that a man becomes is shaped to a large extent by his father. Young people tend to be influenced most by the parent of the same gender. Sometimes fathers are role models: An outgoing father will have an outgoing son; a cautious father will have a careful son; a father who lies may have a liar for a son as well. Other times sons are shaped as a reaction or rejection of their father: A controlling, overbearing father may have a timid, shy son; a scrupulously honest father may have a sneaky, lying son; a father who is proud of his wealth and possessions may have a son who rejects his riches and helps the poor. Either way, however, a son's personality, values, morality, style of solving problems, and emotions are shaped by his interaction with his father.

Personality

Most psychologists agree that a person's personality is shaped by the age of five. Some aspects of personality are thought to be inherited. That is, a person may have a tendency toward being shy or outgoing, fearful or fearless. These genetic tendencies are further shaped by our earliest experiences. If a fearful person has many frightening experiences, he will become even more afraid.

If the same person experiences a supportive and safe environment, his fearfulness will be minimized.

Other psychologists believe that personality is mainly learned. They say that each experience gives a young child a stimulus either to model or to react against. The way the child responds to different aspects of his environment becomes his personality. If personality is mainly learned, then every experience that a young child has with his parents shapes his personality. Thus, his relationship with each parent, mother and father, becomes very important.

Values

Our values are shaped by our father's values: honesty, hard work, intelligence, faith, money, or a sense of humor above all others. The confusion arises when a father says that he values one thing but his actions tell a different story. A father may say that honesty is the most important thing in his life, yet he may cheat on his taxes, be dishonest when making out expense reports, or deny speeding when stopped by a police officer. Another father may say that he values his family more than anything else, yet find excuses to spend most of his time away from home.

When words and actions don't match, it is confusing. Sons often accuse their fathers of being hypocrites. The fact is that few people really think carefully about their values. Sometimes values collide. A father may value his son above all else but still feel that he deserves punishment when he has done something wrong. The most honest man may sometimes keep his opinions to himself to avoid hurting another's feelings.

Morality

Morality is a system of right and wrong. Societies, churches, and families all have their own standards of right and wrong. Each person eventually decides on his own standards.

Sons learn about right and wrong from their fathers, sometimes through a system of punishments:

"If you get home late, you will be grounded."
"If you get a D on your report card, you will lose your phone privileges."
"One more speeding ticket, and we're cancelling the insurance."

Other times the question of right and wrong is more emotional:

"If my dad finds out, he'll kill me."
"I'll have to listen to an hour-long lecture when Dad sees my report card."
"Sure, Dad smacked me, but it's OK. You should have heard what I said to him first."

These paternal reactions are not discussed and agreed upon ahead of time, but the sons understand and expect them.

Morality, like values, can sometimes be contradictory. Sometimes a church's morality may not match that of society. For example, a movie that most people would consider acceptable may be considered pornographic by some churches. Birth control and abortion may be considered moral by society but immoral by some religious groups. If churches and governments can't agree on right and wrong, it's no wonder that a person's moral beliefs may be contradictory.

Problem-Solving

Sons learn a great deal about how to solve everyday problems from observing their father. Some men make excuses, blame others, or pretend that the problem didn't really happen. Other men face up to problems, accept responsibility when they are wrong, and go out of their way to help other people during difficult times. All of these behaviors influence sons.

The best way to understand how your father solves problems is to discuss the issue directly. Ask him why he did what he did. Was there an alternative? Why was this the best way to solve the problem? This will help you to form your own ways of solving everyday problems.

Some social scientists believe that behind the recent increase in teenage suicides is the fact that adolescents have no strategies for facing serious problems. Instead of confronting a problem and considering all the alternatives, they see death as the only escape. Thinking and talking about how to face up to and solve problems is a good way to stay safe from suicidal ideas.

Emotional Closeness or Distance

Children learn about expressing themselves and their feelings from their parents, particularly their same-gender parent. Emotionally closed fathers tend to have sons who are also guarded emotionally. Fathers who are not afraid to show and share their feelings are better able to pass this trait on to their children.

If you feel emotionally distant from your father and are also guarded emotionally, there are a few things that you can do. First, take the risk of trying to communicate emotionally and honestly with your father, even if you have never been able to do so before. It will require patience, stubbornness, and even a little bit of courage. But if you are successful it will do you both a world of good.

If this does not help, learn to open up to other people such as your mother, your school counselor, a social worker, a youth minister, an aunt or an uncle. Learning to express and share your feelings accurately and honestly will help you later when you become an adult and perhaps some day a father as well.

CHAPTER ◇ 5

Older Fathers

George

Georgge Andropoulos and his father lived in a moderately priced apartment on the city's north side. Last week their apartment seemed more crowded than it ever had before. George's brother and sister were in town, along with his six nieces and nephews. They always had a great time together. The fact that two of George's nieces were older than he seemed strange to some people, but they all felt more like very close cousins. In fact, George felt closer to the six of them than he did to his own brother and sister. After all, his sister, Alexandra, was twenty-two years older than George. Stephen, his brother, was seventeen years older.

George's parents had met and married when his mother was eighteen and his father was twenty-six. They started a family right away. When George's mother turned forty-two her daughter was beginning her own family, her son was finishing high school, and she was surprised to discover that she was pregnant. Although the pregnancy

28

completely changed their thoughts about their "golden years," they happily welcomed baby George into their lives.

When George was ten years old his mother was diagnosed with breast cancer. This was an extremely difficult period for the family. Most of a year was spent traveling between home, a variety of hospitals, and finally a local hospice. Thirteen months after her diagnosis, George's mother died.

Last week Alexandra and Stephen had brought their families to town to celebrate both their father's sixty-fifth birthday and his retirement after working forty-two years for Speros Manufacturing. For a birthday present they had jointly purchased an all-expenses paid vacation for two to Florida. Mr. Andropoulos invited his brother, Gustav, to join him for a week of sun, golf, and sightseeing.

The week at home passed quickly for George. Stephen had business in town, so he stayed at the apartment with George. Each evening Stephen told George stories about their parents when they were young. It was like hearing about people George had never known. His mother had been energetic and full of life. She attended all of Stephen's school activities. She was a Cub Scout den leader for Stephen and a Brownie leader for Alexandra. Stephen told him about the time their father taught him to throw a curve ball.

George had trouble visualizing all this. His experience with his parents had been diametrically different. He remembered his mother gradually becoming sicker until she died. His father spent all his time caring for her and then mourning her. Certainly he was either too busy or too heartsick to teach George to throw a curve ball.

When Mr. Andropoulos returned from Florida he was

more animated than George could ever recall. He and Gustav had had a wonderful trip. So wonderful, in fact, that they had decided to purchase a home in a retirement community a few miles from the Gulf coast. Even though the community was planned for retirees, George would be permitted to live with them.

"After all," Mr. Andropoulos said, "you'll be out of high school in a couple of years. Then you'll be leaving home anyway."

George wondered what it would be like to leave his friends, his home, and his niece and nephews. Seeing his father's happiness, however, he kept his feelings to himself. As much as he hated the idea of moving, he couldn't deny his father's happiness.

George tried to put on a good front after the move. He was the youngest person in the entire community. No other high students lived there. Lack of competition made it easy for George to get a job as a caddy at the golf course, but the isolation of the community made it awfully hard to make friends. Each morning George was picked up for a forty-minute bus ride to Forest High School. Most of the other kids who rode the bus were freshmen. George tried to get to know them, but he didn't have much in common with them.

George didn't see much of his father. Mr. Andropoulos and Uncle Gustav were always golfing or playing cards at the community center. This wouldn't have mattered so much, but there was nothing to do and no one to do it with.

One afternoon George stepped off the bus to see ambulance lights flashing in front of their house and Uncle Gustav talking to a paramedic. Mr. Andropulos had suffered a stroke. As he was strapped into the ambulance, he was conscious, but not fully awake. A half smile crossed his face when he recognized George beside him.

In the hospital waiting room, George and Uncle Gustav were finally able to talk to the doctor. The stroke had paralyzed his legs; he would probably be in a wheelchair for the rest of his life.

In the days after Mr. Andropoulos returned home, Uncle Gustav regularly took his brother to the community center, where they played cards and socialized with the other retirees. In the afternoon, George cared for his father. He cooked, cleaned, ran errands, and did whatever needed to be done.

Mr. Andropoulos was slowly becoming bitter and unhappy. Living in a wheelchair frustrated him. Depending on his son and brother made him feel helpless. His brooding and complaining made it harder each day for George and Gustav to care for him.

George had never felt so alone in his life. He was responsible for caring for both himself and his father. He felt that he was missing his entire adolescence. He desperately wished that someone understood how he felt.

STAGES OF LATER LIFE

Most teenagers' parents are twenty to thirty-five years older than their children. The age difference is equal to the range during which the majority of North American women give birth. Adults aged thirty-five to fifty usually are engaged in whatever has become their lifework. They are generally in the most stable and productive part of their career.

Just as children go through phases from infant to adolescent, adults in later life pass through predictable phases. Some of the problems and worries of later life are the following:

• Health concerns
• Retirement/job change
• Lower energy and activity levels
• Loss of loved ones
• Regrets

Teenagers with older parents may be better able to cope with these difficulties if they understand them better and know what to expect.

Health Concerns

People are living longer than ever before. Diseases that were deadly fifty years ago are treatable now. An important key to good health is monitoring our own bodies for any changes and seeking a doctor's care immediately when needed. Older adults must continually worry that aches and pains may be warning signs of serious illness. They often seem preoccupied with their health. That is understandable, since diseases such as cancer, heart disease, Parkinson's disease, Alzheimer's disease, and many others take years to develop. Slowing or stopping the disease usually requires early diagnosis.

Besides concerns for their own health, many older adults spend a great deal of time caring for spouses, other relatives, and close friends.

Retirement

Although most people dream of a day when they will no longer need to work, many older adults find the transition to retirement very stressful. Losing the daily routine, the contact with coworkers, and the sense of accomplishment in work can create great anxiety. Careful planning can make the transition much easier, but an abrupt change of plans caused by a forced retirement, illness, or a major change of lifestyle can create difficulties for older adults. Many retirees sink their life savings into a community far from friends and family, only to find it hard to get out if they become unhappy with the new home.

Retirement usually is accompanied by a reduced income. Pensions and retirement plans assume that retirees will need less money than when they were raising a family. That means less opportunity for recreation and travel, which can be disappointing for people who expected to be financially comfortable during their retirement.

Lower Energy and Activity Levels

As people age, they tire more easily. Many older adults jog, dance, play tennis and golf, and participate in other physical activities, but they generally find that they must take their exercise a little more easily. This slowing-down process can be very frustrating. Many older adults push themselves too hard while ignoring their bodies' signals of pain and fatigue. Thus they can miss the early warning signals of disease.

Men are particularly prone to resent the slowing down of their body. As so many changes are occurring in their relationships and daily habits, they have trouble accepting that their body is declining as well. It is usually emotionally healthy for retired men to find new interests and pursuits more suited to this phase of their lives.

Loss of Loved Ones

As time passes and friends and relatives die, older adults experience great loss and sadness. They confront thoughts of their own life and death on a regular basis.

A sense of loss is also felt when lifelong friends move away, divorce, or undergo extended hospitalization. These losses are difficult as well. People are able to cope more easily when life is somewhat predictable.

Regret

Another characteristic of older adult years is regret. Some people wish that they had been more successful financially, a better parent, a more loving spouse, or that they had practiced better nutrition or lived a more moral life.

Regret is part of the process that people go through when they evaluate their life. Regret should encourage us to improve our life, forgive others, and love better.

Regret is unhealthy for older adults when they dwell on their shortcomings rather than their accomplishments. They need to move beyond regret to accept and appreciate their life as a whole.

COPING WITH AN OLDER FATHER

Sons and daughters of older fathers can cope best by first understanding that the changes their father undergoes are normal and predictable. Teenagers often find themselves in the role of caretaker for their disabled parent. In such a situation, find out what help is available. Cities, counties, churches, and synagogues have volunteers who help to care for shut-ins and disabled people. Insurance may cover home health care when it is needed. If your father is unaware of such help, talk to his doctor, clergyperson, the local health department, or your school counselor to find out what help is available. If you have brothers or sisters, try to balance the workload so that everyone shares.

Remember that the love and nurturing that our parents gave us when we were infants and children may need to be returned in their later years. Give it as it was given to you, with patience and love.

CHAPTER 6

Fathers Who Have Abandoned Their Family

Justin

Justin never thought too much about it when he was little. He knew that some kids had a father and he didn't. Since he had never had a father, it seemed normal to Justin. When he got into second grade, however, he began to notice how different some kids' families were from his own. Not the tiny apartment and the monthly worry that his mother wouldn't be able to pay the rent. Most of their neighbors faced that same challenge. The difference that Justin noticed was that many of his classmates talked about their fathers.

Once he asked his mother, "Is my father dead?" She answered, "I don't think so."

Justin continued, "Did you get a divorce?" His mother responded honestly, "No, we were never married."

Pressing further, Justin wanted to know, "Where is he? Can I see him?" Sadly, his mother replied, "I don't know where he is. The last time I talked to him was before you were even born, he left us so long ago. Now, I don't even want to see him again."

That was many years ago. Now at the age of fifteen, Justin sometimes feels sad about his life. He wonders: Why did he leave us? Was there something wrong with him? Is there something wrong with my mother that would make him leave her? Is there something wrong with me that made my father abandon us?

Marlena

Marlena didn't need anyone to tell her that she was different. Her mother, stepfather, half brothers, and half sister were all freckle-faced, strawberry blonds who sunburned easily. Marlena had black hair, dark brown eyes, and skin that tanned to a golden brown. A guy at school, showing more curiosity than sensitivity, asked, "Are you Mexican or Puerto Rican?" Instead of answering, Marlena simply gave him an icy glare.

Marlena was the oldest of the children. The others, including her mother, Patty, had the same last name, Murphy. Marlena's last name was Fernandez. When she was twelve, Marlena's stepfather had asked her if she would like him to adopt her; then her last name would be Murphy like the rest of the family. At the time Marlena wanted no part of the idea. She was beginning to develop a sense of independence. She was used to being different and was determined to go through life that way.

When she was fourteen, however, Marlena told her mother that she was going to find her real father. She was tired of being different and wanted to be with him. She demanded to know his name, where he lived, and why he had left. Patty gave her the best answer she could: His name was Willie Fernandez; she had no idea where he lived; and his leaving was for everybody's good.

Patty confessed that when they first started out together, she and Willie were only seventeen. They tried drugs, marijuana and cocaine, together. Willie seemed to like drugs more than she did. She had stopped using them about two months before she found out that she was pregnant. Willie was starting to use more and more. Patty and Willie lived together for six months after their baby was born. Finally, she told Willie that he would have to choose between drugs and her. That was the last night that they were together.

Twice when Marlena was little Willie tried to get back together again, but he couldn't kick his drug habit. By the second time he tried to reconcile, Patty had already become involved with Marlena's stepfather. She told Willie not to come back. For eleven years he had done just that.

Mike

Mike was quick-tempered and argumentative. He fought with his mother, his teachers, his sister, and just about anyone else who was willing to fight back. His mother told him that he was just like his father, never satisfied with anyone or anything. She said she had thought that the house would be calmer after his father left two years ago, but Mike had just picked up where his father had left off.

Mike was so furious at his mother's comments that he burst out of the house. He knew that he needed to cool off, to think. He had a quiet place in a nearby park where he went on occasions like this. Unfortunately, the need to cool off came all too frequently.

Mike thought that maybe he *was* just like his father. When they had gone hunting and fishing a few times, Mike remembered, he had had to be careful to do exactly what his father told him. He didn't want to make him angry. He clearly remembered the reaction when he accidentally spilled a can of Coke into a box of shotgun shells. His father yelled and carried on for the rest of the trip. He was still calling Mike a "klutz" six months later.

Since he left, Mike's father called Mike on his birthday and a couple of other times. They talked about getting together sometime but didn't make any firm plans. Each time his mother took the phone when Mike was finished. He heard her say, "I'm not raising these kids all by myself. You better start sending me some money for child support pretty soon. If you don't. I'll see you in court."

Each phone conversation ended with Mike's father hanging up on her and Mike's mother crying at the kitchen table.

COPING WITH ABANDONMENT

Fathers abandoning their families has become increasingly common recently. More single mothers and married mothers are raising children on their own than at any time in history. Children in these families struggle to understand why their father left. It is easier for them to cope if they can find an answer to that question.

Conflict Within Himself

Generally when fathers abandon their family they have some kind of internal conflict. They may blame the children or the mother, but the responsibility for failure is their own.

Some men start a family before they are ready to fulfill such a commitment. Parenting requires hard work and maturity. Young fathers are sometimes unable to put aside their own wants and needs for the good of their wife and children. They think they can simply walk away, forgetting that their family still need food, shelter, and medical care. Fathers who say that they left because they "just weren't ready to start a family" are not living up to their responsibility for lives they brought into the world.

Sometimes a young father is unable to support a family financially. He may not have enough education to earn the money to maintain a home. Many young men have not learned to budget their money to pay the monthly bills. Judges usually require a father to contribute some money to his children even if his income is very low.

Sometimes young fathers have difficulty remaining faithful sexually. Both married and unmarried parents need a core-of respect for each other and a shared commitment to keep the family strong and healthy. A father who is having sexual affairs with other women is seldom able to maintain such a commitment.

Another conflict that causes fathers to abandon their family is addiction to alcohol, drugs, or gambling. Addiction is a disease. Left untreated, it becomes worse until its victim dies. No one is strong enough to break an addiction without help.

It is important for the family of an alcoholic or drug addict to avoid making the addict's problem everyone's problem. This sharing is called **codependency**. A codependent changes his or her life in important ways so that the addict can continue to indulge in his habit.

Sometimes it is necessary to force an addict to make a

choice either to get help or to leave the family. Many fathers choose to abandon their family. In some cases this step helps the addict to realize how serious his situation is and to seek treatment. It may seem harsh to see one's father being told to leave. But the purpose is to push the addict into treatment, *not* out of the family. Getting help for the addict is the only way for the family to recover.

Many addicted fathers choose their disease over their family. Some seek treatment years after abandoning their family. Sadly, the family may have recovered in his absence. When he wants to return, they may not accept him.

Conflicts with Mother

Some men claim that they abandoned their family because they could not get along with the children's mother. In a court, this is called "irreconcilable differences." It means that the two adults will never be able to maintain a relationship that will allow them to live together as a family.

Irreconcilable differences is a common cause for divorce, but it is not an acceptable excuse for abandonment. People do make unsuitable romantic choices, but when a baby is a result of such a choice the father and mother are responsible for the child even if they are living apart. Adults divorce one another, but only a judge can remove their rights and responsibilities as parents.

Conflicts with Children

Some fathers claim that they have found they simply are not good parents. This sometimes happens. It takes wisdom and maturity to face up to one's failures as a person. However, being a poor parent does not take away the father's responsibility to support his children as best he can. A father with a low income is expected to contribute what he can to his family. In the same way, a father with little to contribute emotionally is obliged to give what he can to his children.

It is not the responsibility of a child to make a parent feel better about himself. A baby cannot contribute to his parents' self-esteem. A toddler cannot provide care and understanding. A parent needs to *give* love to his young children. The love that a young child receives from his parents at an early age helps him to be better able to care for others as he gets older.

Self-Esteem

Many children who have been abandoned by their fathers lack self-esteem. You can improve your self-esteem by following these steps:

Appreciate the family that you do have. Dwelling on the loss of your father will not accomplish much. By appreciating your mother, siblings, and other people in your home, you can feel better about the family that you do have. Single-parent families created by divorce or death face many of the same challenges that your family faces.

Don't idealize your father. Learn what you can about your father, and try to accept him as he is. If he is unable to meet his commitment to his family, try to accept that. If addiction is keeping him from you, understand that addiction is a disease that needs professional treatment.

Don't search for your father. Searching for your father or trying to rejoin him after he has abandoned your family simply makes you a codependent. Leaving your family to join him will make whatever problem he has your problem too.

Find healthy role models for yourself. Any child growing up in a single-parent family needs role models of both genders. Scout leaders, coaches, teachers, ministers, and other trustworthy adults can help teenagers learn to develop the skills and responsibilities that they will need as young adults and later as parents.

CHAPTER 7

Fathers Who Work

Away from Home

The Rinder Family

I t was a no-win situation for the Rinders. Economic times were tough in their part of the country. After substitute-teaching for five years. Mrs. Rinder finally was offered a full-time job. She loved teaching, and the money really helped. This was her dream job. After raising the children and paying her dues as a substitute teacher, she didn't want to start over.

Mr. Rinder wasn't given too many alternatives: He could either accept a transfer out of state or start looking for another job. The Rinders talked until late at night trying to decide what to do. In the end they decided to try to do both. Mr. Rinder would accept the transfer and look for a new job in their hometown at the same time. Admittedly it would be hard to do while working out of state, but he would try his best.

Their plan was for him to rent a one-bedroom

apartment and fly home on the weekends. He could call home every night. In the meantime, Mrs. Rinder would keep her job and keep Kevin and Sean with her at home.

The two boys took the news in stride. They all agreed that if they pulled together, the family could make it work.

Two weeks later the entire family drove Mr. Rinder to the airport. They all pretended that it was just another business trip, but each of them knew that their family was about to change dramatically. Dad made small talk with each of his boys. He spoke to Kevin about his classes at North High School. He and Sean talked about the upcoming science fair at Franklin Middle School. Dad reminded them that he would call every night.

The first two nights Dad called at exactly 9 o'clock. He talked to each of them. His new job was very exciting, and he was putting in very long hours. He said that he had an evening meeting on Wednesday, so he wouldn't call again until Thursday. Thursday night he called at 9:15. They mostly talked about arrangements for Mrs. Rinder to pick him up on Friday.

Friday night they all went out to dinner. Everyone seemed to be talking at once. Mom and Kevin were both telling Dad about the article Kevin had written for the school newspaper. Sean tried to listen politely, but no one really was paying attention to him. He tried to make a few jokes until Kevin told him to shut up.

Kevin did just that. If no one cared how his science fair project was coming along, he wouldn't bring it up. After all, it wasn't coming along at all. His dad usually helped Sean with projects.

The next week Mr. Rinder had an even harder time calling home. Twice he was too late to talk to the boys. Mr. Rinder told his wife that he would try to spend some time with the boys on the weekend, but that it would be hard, since he would be bringing work home with him.

Kevin decided not to join the swim team this year. He knew he could make varsity, but it would take up time that he needed to help out at home. After a few days, however, Kevin realized that he had more free time than he had expected. His friend Jack liked to work on cars, so Kevin started hanging out with him. Mrs. Rinder was so busy with teaching and taking care of the house that she hardly noticed that Kevin wasn't around very much.

On Friday of the fourth week after Mr. Rinder had started his new job, Mrs. Rinder received a call from Kevin's school. The dean had caught Kevin cutting classes with Jack. Kevin explained that they needed to get a part for Jack's car.

Mr. Rinder came on strong with Kevin. He grounded his son for the next week and ordered him to come directly home from school each day. Kevin argued that the punishment was unfair. His father answered: "I don't care. I expected you to be *more* responsible, not less."

On Monday afternoon when Mrs. Rinder got home from school, she found that Kevin wasn't home yet. An hour later Kevin walked in. His mother demanded, "Where were you? You know that you're grounded."

Kevin simply replied, "That was Dad's punishment. I didn't think it was fair."

Kevin and his mother had a long, heated discussion. Finally she called Mr. Rinder. His tone with Kevin on the phone was far from calm. After hanging up, Kevin stormed out of the house.

Mrs. Rinder called her husband back. "I need you here," she pleaded.

He promised to come home Thursday night, but she

said Thursday was too late. Mr. Rinder answered meekly. "I'll see what I can do."

Wednesday morning Mrs. Rinder looked at the weekly calendar. "Sean," she asked, "wasn't last night the science fair? What happened?"

Sean hung his head. "My project stinks. I tried to do it by myself, but it kept falling apart. With all the trouble that you were having with Kevin, I didn't want to bother you. I won a first-place ribbon last year. I couldn't have done better anyway, so why should I even try?"

DISTANCE PULLS FAMILIES APART

Families with one parent working away from home find it difficult to maintain the balance and stability that they once enjoyed. Many experience feelings similar to those following a divorce or death. Loss, sadness, and loneliness are common. Each family member needs to assume certain roles when the father is away and different ones when he returns.

Coming back together on weekends can be stressful too. Families can become accustomed to having one member away. But having one regularly leaving and returning can be very disruptive to family rules and patterns of communication.

When a father works away from home, his wife feels the added responsibility of raising a family like a single parent. Adults are happiest and cope best when they are in a relationship with another significant adult. Single parents need to develop this relationship outside of the family, sometimes with a close friend, an adult sibling, or in a romantic relationship. When a father is away from home most of the time, it places great stress on the marital relationship. Both need time to communicate regularly, and when the family is reunited, they need private time together to rebuild and strengthen their relationship.

It is important for families to understand that the parents' relationship is a priority. When all their time is occupied with the problems of the children, they are less able to work together as a family. Although the feelings and needs of each family member are important, it is essential that the parents be able to work together.

Compromise

When a father works away from home, everyone needs to compromise. Discussion of future plans and privileges needs to be delayed until the weekend or whenever the father returns. Daily chores and projects need to be done during the week so that the weekend is free. When possible, minor problems should be solved as they come up, so that serious matters can be addressed when the family is reunited.

It is a rare family that prefers to have a father working out of town. Resentment can build, since the members have limitations that other families don't have. Dad cannot attend weekday school functions and sporting events. He is not available to help with homework and projects. Having to share the precious together time can lead to resentment by each family member.

Compromise can also lead to anger. Children and teenagers expect parents to set limits. When those limits are suddenly removed, it is too easy to experiment with new behaviors, such as Kevin tried by cutting class. In most families, consequences for breaking family rules are immediate, short, and fair. A father working away from home isn't available to assess the seriousness of the situation.

Not all divided families are able to be reunited every weekend. Geologists, truck drivers, merchant mariners, military people, and many others must make long stays away from home. Family members need to concentrate on working together. They should speak frankly and try to understand one another's needs.

Staying Close When Time Is Short

It is possible to stay close when your father works away from home. You may want to try these four steps:

Ask your father for personal time together. Tell him clearly, "There is something that I need to talk to you about. When would be a good time?"

Get to the point. When time is short, don't waste it beating around the bush. Discuss the topic in a straightforward and honest way. Avoid side issues, and don't try to make your father feel guilty. He is probably just as unhappy about being away from home as you are. Have a plan for what you want to say. This will help you to stick to the main topic and explain it clearly. Sometimes thinking a problem through thoroughly will let you find the solution on your own. You think. "If I say . . . , he'll probably say . . . " This may help you to work out the entire problem. If it does, tell your father about it anyway.

Learn your father's schedule. Knowing that you can get in touch with your father if necessary can be very comforting. You may decide not to call him with a problem, but it will help to know that you could.

Support your mother. Your mother may be finding it hard to live most of the week without your father. Your patience and understanding can help her a great deal. You don't need to become "the man of the house." But taking the initiative to do chores and cooperate can make it much easier to function as a family when you are together on the weekends.

Remember that people cope best when they are in a situation that they understand. Communication and cooperation are the keys to coping as a family whose father works away from home.

CHAPTER ◇ 8

Imprisoned Fathers

Maurice

t was the third fight that Maurice had had in two weeks. Eighth-graders can be cruel. When they discover something that will make a guy lose control, they sometimes stir things up just for the fun of it. Ever since the papers started covering the trial of Maurice's father for selling stolen goods, his classmates had been merciless.

Some taunted him about what was happening to his father in jail. They made jokes about all those men together in close quarters. Maurice was infuriated at their insinuations about his father in sexual situations with other men. That was how two of the fights had started.

Others made references to Maurice himself. "Don't let Maurice use your book; he'll probably sell it." A boy in science class suggested that they should search Maurice for a missing calculator, because stolen merchandise was in his genes, a pun on "jeans."

Maurice's mother lost a half day's pay when she went to the school to take Maurice home after the third fight. The principal was very sympathetic. He said he understood her difficulty and would ask the teachers to be more understanding of Maurice's situation.

And indeed the teachers did seem to treat him differently when he returned from his suspension. Mr. Milliken, his science teacher, moved Maurice's seat to the front and center of the classroom. When Maurice asked to borrow equipment to complete some of his missing work, Mr. Milliken made him sign for it. During a test, Mr. Milliken told him three times to keep his eyes on his own paper but never said a thing to the other students.

Mrs. Wilson welcomed Maurice back to English class and told him not to worry about the work that he had missed. She said she knew he was a smart boy and would catch up easily. The day's lesson was about using pronouns correctly in sentences. Maurice didn't understand the concept. He raised his hand and asked Mrs. Wilson to explain. She responded, "Don't worry about it, honey, it isn't that important."

He could hear a taunting chorus of whispers from the students around him, "Maurice, honey, don't worry." He didn't know what bothered him most, the teasing or the fact that Mrs. Wilson wasn't taking him seriously.

Maurice tried to tell his mother what was happening at school, but she was distracted. The bills, her job, his two sisters, and the next three to five years without a husband were all weighing heavily on her mind. She told Maurice that she loved him very much, but that she didn't know how they were going to make it while his father was in prison.

The next day Maurice noticed that his mother's spirits had lifted a little. She said she had wonderful news: They would be able to visit his father at the prison on the weekend.

Maurice wasn't sure if this was wonderful news at all. The prison frightened him. He knew that there were dangerous men there, and he really didn't want to go near them. It never occurred to him that many of the men might be a lot like his father.

Maurice was divided in his feelings about his father. On one hand he was continually defending him. Until the judge pronounced sentence, Maurice maintained that his father was innocent. Now he said, "So what! People break the law every day. This was no big deal."

Yet while he was defending his father, inside he felt embarrassed and betrayed. "How could he care so little about us? All my problems at school and all Momma's problems are his fault. Why did he do this to us?"

On Saturday Maurice, his mother, and his sisters drove to the prison. They passed armed guards at the gate and saw the guard towers and the security fences. After parking the car, they had to walk through metal detectors to get into the building. The guard emptied his mother's purse on a table for everyone to see. His mother didn't do anything wrong. Why were they treating her like a criminal?

They were taken into a room divided in half by a long table. The prisoners were on one side, the families on the other. Maurice's little sister Laticia rushed ahead to hug her father. The guard stopped her and said brusquely, "No physical contact!"

They were allowed to sit across the table and talk, but they were not allowed to touch. Other families were on each side of them, denying them any chance to have a private conversation. Maurice's parents talked about prison, home, her work, money, and what it would be like in three to five years when they were back together again. Maurice and his sisters didn't say a word. Marla was too afraid, Laticia was too angry, and Maurice didn't know how to put his feelings into words.

HOW TO HANDLE YOUR FEELINGS

Having a father in prison raises a variety of confusing emotions. Three common feelings that teenagers experience are confusion, betrayal, and anger.

Confusion

It is hard to understand having one's own father sent to prison. Most people grow up with an image of how life is "supposed to be." They think of their parents as the people who teach them to distinguish right from wrong. When a parent is put on trial and sent to prison, his child's ideas about right and wrong become confused. Was my father right and the judge wrong? Were the things that my father taught me were right actually wrong? Were the things he taught me were wrong actually right?

Sorting out these issues becomes very important for the children of imprisoned fathers. It helps to understand that no person is always good or always evil. Good people make serious mistakes at times. That does not make them "bad" people. If you think about what you know to be right from school, church, your mother, or other important adults in your life, it can help you to find the good in a father who has been sent to prison.

Betrayal

Another common feeling is betrayal. Family members feel that their father has let them down. They expected him to be there for them, and he won't be for a long time. They expected to be able to talk proudly about their father, and now people are making them feel ashamed of him. They expected him to provide for the family, and now money is tighter than ever. The first step in coping with feelings of betrayal is to admit them to yourself. Then you may want to share your feelings with someone you trust: your mother, a guidance counselor, social worker, clergyperson, or a close aunt or uncle.

Anger

A third common feeling is anger. It may be directed at teachers at school, the police who arrested your father, your mother, or any other convenient target. Like the feeling of betrayal, it is important to recognize anger and express it to someone you can trust.

Anger may also be a more direct result of the crime. Crimes such as child abuse, neglect, or failure to provide child support are hard to understand and accept because the victim is the family itself.

HOW TO HANDLE COMMENTS

Having a father in prison is not an easy secret to keep. People may have seen the arrest. The news of the trial may have been in the paper or on television. Friends innocently ask, Where is your father? People react differently to imprisonment.

Many people ridicule what they don't understand, and having a father in prison is hard to understand. Other people poke fun to make themselves feel superior by tearing down someone else. It is easier to cope with teasing and ridicule if you understand its purpose. No one who makes fun of a father in prison really deserves an explanation; but if you decide to give one, make it factual and straightforward. If people understand the situation, they may no longer find it funny.

Another reaction is mistrust. People feel that if your father did something wrong, you must be untrustworthy as well. This is completely unfair, but very common. Often it helps to confront the mistrustful person calmly and say, "You need to judge me for myself. What my father does should not influence the way you treat me."

Some people react by being overly sympathetic, or patronizing. A patronizing person heaps kindness on you without listening to your wants, needs, or opinions. Try to connect with such people directly and honestly. Ask them to stop for a moment and listen to you. Let them know that you want to be treated fairly rather than "specially."

A VISIT TO PRISON

Visiting a father in prison can be a frightening experience. All the prisoners have been sent there for breaking a law. They must follow strict rules. Armed guards throughout the prison and in watchtowers keep order. Visitors sometimes try to sneak contraband—drugs, alcohol, weapons—to prisoners, so elaborate procedures are used to prevent this. Metal detectors and pat-down searches are commonly utilized, and prisoners are not allowed to touch visitors.

Having a picture in your mind of what it will be like to visit the prison will make the experience less frightening. People can more easily cope with things that they expect and understand.

Trying to share your feelings with your father in prison may be very difficult at first. It may take a few visits before you are able to express yourself honestly and calmly.

Be patient with yourself. More than likely you will have many months to say the things you really want to say. Sometimes it's easier to put your feelings in a letter. If you do, and if you are still feeling confused, angry, or betrayed, hold onto the letter for a day and reread it. Make sure it says what you really want to say.

Finally, visit as often as you can. If your father has a long sentence, it will still help to visit. Avoiding him will make the hurt last longer. Visits can support him and help you. If the visits hurt and confuse you, find a trusted person to help you sort things out. Most prisons provide family support groups. Encourage everyone in your family to join such a group.

CHAPTER 9

Gay Fathers

Sara

A t first Sara thought it was strange, but later it made sense. When her parents sat down with her and her brother Zack two years ago to tell them that they were getting a divorce, she was shocked. Her parents had always seemed to get along, they didn't argue, and they talked about growing old together. She couldn't understand why they would want to get a divorce.

Their only explanation at the time was that they cared about each other but could not stay married. All kinds of ideas went through Sara's mind. Was her father having an affair? Her mother? Was her father doing something illegal? Did one of them lose a lot of money in a bad investment? Although Sara was only thirteen, she figured that the breakup had to be over either sex or money.

After the divorce, Sara and Zack lived with their mother. Most weekends they spent at their father's apartment. It seemed that their mother tried to restrict the time they spent there, but she did let them go.

A few months later their mother told them that she was

going to begin dating again. Sara and Zack had mixed feelings about that. They wanted her to be happy, but her dating seemed to make the divorce more final. It would be hard for their parents ever to get back together if they were involved with other people.

Their father didn't seem interested in dating at all. To save money, he was sharing an apartment with Jim, an old friend of his. Although Dad didn't have any new women in his life, he didn't seem lonely either. He told them about movies that he and Jim had seen and restaurants in the neighborhood that they both liked.

One day Sara got a call from Jim, who said that her father had been in an accident and was in the hospital. When Sara and Zack walked into the hospital room, they saw their father lying in bed while Jim held his hand and stroked his forehead. Sara thought her father must have been hurt seriously for Jim to show so much concern, but Dad turned and smiled. "They're just keeping me for observation. I'll be able to leave in a few hours."

The next weekend, when Sara and Zack went to their father's place, he acted nervous. He seemed to want to say something but didn't know how to start. Finally after dinner he asked them to sit on the couch; there was something he wanted to discuss with them.

"What I am about to tell you may shock you or hurt you. I know it disturbed your mother when I first told her. It's the reason that we had to divorce.

"This is hard, so I'll come right out and say it. I'm gay. I am a homosexual. I guess I always knew it but didn't want to face up to it. Marrying your mother was a way of running away from being gay, but it didn't work.

"I didn't choose to be gay. It's the way I am and the way I always will be. Jim I are very happy together. We are very quiet about our homosexuality. We don't march in parades or tell the people that we work with, but we decided it was time for you to know."

Sara didn't know how to react. She was trying to re-assemble the last few years in her mind. A lot of things made sense now. She understood why her mother had started dating, but her father hadn't. Although the revelation did disturb her, it was all starting to make sense.

Zack, on the other hand, became eerily quiet. He didn't respond directly, but walked into the next room. He turned on the television and stared fixedly at it. His father sat down beside him and asked, "Do you want to talk about it?"

Zack snarled, "No, I want to go *home*. I don't ever want to come here again. You're a faggot, a queer. I'm not like you. I don't ever want to see you again."

SEXUAL ORIENTATION

Humans are oriented to be sexually attracted to the opposite gender or to the same gender. Persons primarily attracted to members of the opposite sex are called heterosexual. Persons attracted to their own sex, male or female, are called homosexual. Some people are attracted to both their own sex and the opposite sex. These people are called bisexual.

There is much controversy as to whether sexual orientation is chosen, learned, or inherited. One school of thought holds that sexual orientation is chosen. People choose to be homosexual or heterosexual, and they could abandon their orientation simply by choosing another orientation. The argument against this theory is that people who have tried to change sexual orientation have had a great deal of difficulty. People do not control their sexual attraction to another person. Sexual attraction is emotional, not rational. The majority of homosexuals say that if they had a choice they would never choose a gay lifestyle.

Another school of thought is that sexual orientation is learned at an early age. Our experiences with adult role models, how we play, and our first senses of intimate touching all lead us toward a heterosexual or homosexual orientation. This theory holds that what is taught can be untaught or retaught. That is, a person can learn to change his sexual orientation. The argument against this theory is that personality is also set and determined at an early age. Since people cannot change their personality to any great extent, they cannot change their sexual orientation either. As for preventing homosexuality through early learning, the people who believe that sexual orientation is mainly learned have not been able to identify the factors in a young child's life that lead to a homosexual orientation.

More recently evidence has been mounting that homosexuality is inherited genetically. New research has isolated a gene specifically linked to men with a homosexual orientation. Geneticists believe that sexual orientation can be identified through a blood or tissue test. This theory is still in its infancy, and it does not completely explain how sexual sttraction for another person can be controlled genetically.

HOMOSEXUALITY IN SOCIETY

Homosexuality is not accepted by the majority of people in our society. Religion plays an important role in this lack of acceptance. Christianity, Judaism, and many other religions teach that homosexuality is sinful. They justify prejudice and bigotry against homosexuals on the ground that homosexuality is against God's teachings.

Some mainstream Christian churches have been changing their stand on homosexuality. Some have stated that homosexuality is not sinful. Others still consider homosexual acts sinful, but they want church members to fight for equal rights and social justice for people with a homosexual orientation. These churches no longer condone discrimination against homosexuals.

Many people believe that children should be safeguarded from homosexual day-care workers, teachers, doctors, and other helping professionals. This belief is rooted in the idea that homosexuals are likely to molest young children. Actually, crime statistics show that homosexuals are no more likely to molest children than are heterosexuals. People who are sexually attracted to children are called **pedophiles**. Pedophilia has no relationship whatsoever to sexual orientation.

AIDS

Acquired immunodeficiency syndrome (AIDS) first flourished in North America in the homosexual communities of major metropolitan areas. Because of this, AIDS has come to be thought of as a homosexual disease. Actually, the rate of increase in AIDS cases has been much greater among heterosexual males and females than among homosexuals.

People often use AIDS as another excuse for discriminating against homosexuals. This is unfair, since gays are no more likely than nongays to spread AIDS. The vast majority of scientists are firmly convinced that the virus believed to carry AIDS, HIV, can be transmitted only through sexual contact or blood-to-blood contact. People do not contract AIDS by talking to, eating with, or shaking hands with an infected person.

COPING WITH A HOMOSEXUAL FATHER

With all the prejudice in our society against homosexuality, teenagers with a homosexual father may find it difficult to cope. A first question that many teens ask is, Does this mean that I will be homosexual, too? The little research that has been done on this subject seems to show that children of homosexuals are no more likely to have a homosexual orientation than is the average person.

Coping usually comes from understanding. Sexual orientation is either very difficult or impossible to change. Reading as much as you can about human sexuality may help you to cope. Try to talk to your father. Don't be afraid to ask him questions that will help you understand.

Many teens react angrily to the news that their parent is homosexual. If you find yourself angry with your father, talk to someone who listens well and can help you. Your mother, school counselor, social worker, youth minister, an aunt, uncle, or grandparent are good choices.

Talking to Your Father

Talking to your father is important, too. You need to be careful about what you ask. Parents, both homosexual and heterosexual, are uncomfortable talking about their sexual relationships and experiences. Be sure to respect your father's privacy if he seems uncomfortable talking about his homosexuality.

You might want to ask your father:

• How and when did you know that your sexual orientation was gay?

- How is your lifestyle different from "straight" people?
- How does your sexual preference affect your feelings about me, my mother, and my siblings?

The answers to these questions may help you to understand your own sexual feelings. Certainly the more you understand your father, the more likely it is that you will be able to bridge any emotional distance caused by his homosexuality.

CHAPTER 10

Physically Challenged Fathers

Gerald

Gerald Oldham was a district sales manager for a snack chip company. One cold January day his car hit a patch of sheer ice on a country road. The collision with a forty-foot oak tree resulted in severe back injuries. By the time Gerald's wife, Sally, and his two daughters, Lisa and Chelsea, arrived at the hospital, the doctors had done all that they would be able to do.

The doctor took the family aside and told them that Gerald would live, but that he would never walk again. The force of the impact had severed his spinal cord. Gerald would be in a wheelchair for the rest of his life.

Each family member accepted the news differently. Gerald's main concern was about how he would be able to support his family. He had always expected to be able to provide for them, and now that seemed unlikely. His job had required him to travel in a six-county area servicing his accounts. Fortunately, Gerald's boss told him that a desk job was waiting. He would be working regular hours for the same pay. This was a great relief for Gerald.

Sally was grateful that her husband was alive, but she knew that their lives together had been changed dramatically. The physical closeness that they had always enjoyed now would include her helping Gerald into bed, into the car, into the bathtub, and back into the wheelchair. All these new responsibilities frightened her. She had always relied on Gerald to take care of her. Now, much of the time he would need to depend on Sally.

Lisa was eight years old. She was just happy that Daddy was going to be OK. She asked him if she could ride in the wheelchair with him. Before Gerald could answer, Chelsea cried, "Lisa, how could you say that? Dad isn't in a wheelchair just so you can have fun!"

Gerald quickly broke in, "It's all right, Lisa. We all know this isn't for fun, but when I'm ready you can ride with me."

Chelsea frowned. She thought it was all so unfair. Why is my father going to be in a wheelchair? He didn't do anything wrong. What did he do to deserve this?

Charles

Charles asked his dad if he could go to Myron's house. His dad answered, "Of c . . . c . . . course, Ch . . . Ch . . . Charles. B . . . Be b . . . b . . . ack by f . . . f . . . f . . . five."

Charles replied. "Thanks, Dad." He strolled out the front door.

Myron, Charles, and some other guys from the neighborhood were going to play a little basketball.

Charles was friends with most of the guys there. As a matter of fact, he was friends with every guy in the neighborhood except Martin. Martin was always putting people down. Today he had a new name for Charles: Son of Fudd. Charles asked him, "Why do you call me that?"

Martin taunted him, "Isn't your father Elmer Fudd? Th . . . Th . . . Th . . . That's all folks!"

Charles didn't say anything right then. He wanted to tell Martin that he had his cartoon characters mixed up. Elmer Fudd's speech problem is that he is unable to make the "r" sound. It's Porky Pig who stutters.

However, Charles did take his anger out on Martin once they got on the basketball court. After a few obvious fouls against Martin, the guys on Charles's team asked him to take it easy. "Don't listen to Martin. He's always running off his big old mouth."

The comments and remarks did bother Charles, though. His father had explained to Charles that he had spent many hours and thousands of dollars trying to cure himself of stuttering. Doctors, speech therapists, and even a psychiatrist had not been able to help very much. Everyone in the family understood and accepted his father's stuttering, but it was hard to get other people to understand.

William

Frank Chung had rare talents. He could type ninety words a minute. He could play the piano and just about any other keyboard instrument expertly. His clay sculptures captured the essence of every object that he portrayed. Making all this even more remarkable was the fact that Frank Chung was completely blind.

Frank learned to play the piano by ear. He simply

touched the keys to make the music that he heard. He is now able to use a computer to combine his own creativity with words and music. His recordings and musical compositions allow him to support his wife and three children.

Frank's children, Robert, William, and Edward, are all sighted. Each has taken piano lessons and has been encouraged to learn to use the computer. All three enjoy music, but each has his own interests. William Chung's interest is in baseball.

William has tried to share his interest in baseball with his father, but he can't describe the game well enough for his father to visualize the plays. They have tried listening to games together on the radio, but Frank eventually loses interest. Other boys go to their fathers for tips on hitting or fielding or bunting, but William knows that his father cannot help him with any of these.

William tries not to feel sorry for himself, but sometimes he feels that it just isn't right. It seems unfair that his father can't take him to baseball games, watch him play, or teach him to play better. William sometimes wonders what it would be like if he had a different father.

PHYSICAL CHALLENGES DO NOT CAUSE EMOTIONAL DISTANCE

Physical disabilities have no relationship whatever to how close a father can be to his children. Physically challenged parents are often warm, caring, and very close to their children. However, just as there are physical barriers that these parents must overcome to lead a normal life, so there are barriers to emotional closeness that physically challenged parents must overcome as well.

Dependence versus Independence

The first emotional barrier that physically challenged parents must work out is dependence on family members to do routine things for them. Everyone in a family needs to share in the responsibility of doing what he can to keep a house orderly, safe, and in good repair. Some family members are better suited for some jobs better than others. A three-year-old may be expected to put her toys away, but not to repair a leaky roof. In the same way, there are many contributions that a physically challenged adult cannot make. Blind adults cannot drive. Deaf people need a special apparatus including a keyboard to answer the telephone. An adult in a wheelchair would be stumped in an effort to shovel snow off the steps.

However, the contributions that each family member makes are usually agreed upon and worked out together. One person may like to mow the lawn but hate to do dishes. Another person may like to do the grocery shopping, but dislike vacuuming. Deciding who does what jobs around the house requires everyone to decide: What needs to be done? Who *can* do that job? Which person likes that job the most (or dislikes it the least)? Is everyone doing his fair share?

In a family with a physically challenged parent, many of the necessary chores are different from those in other families. Wheelchair assistance, running errands, making telephone calls, purchasing medical supplies, and other tasks may need to be shared by all members of the family. The physically challenged parent depends on the family to do those things that he is unable to do or that would require extraordinary effort.

Independence is also necessary, however, for everyone in the family. No one feels comfortable when other people do things for him that he could easily do for himself. People lose self-respect when waited upon unnecessarily. All members of a family need to feel that they are making a contribution. Doing your part is an important aspect of being part of a family.

Understanding Physical Challenges

Another barrier to emotional closeness is failure to understand physical challenges. Those who have been blind or deaf all their lives perceive the world very differently from people who hear and see. People with little contact with physically challenged people often avoid them or criticize them simply through lack of understanding.

Some children with a physically challenged parent suffer when their peers ridicule their parent's disability. It may help a little to know that the ridicule comes from ignorance. Many people try to tear down and criticize things that they don't understand. Sometimes it helps to explain the nature of the physical challenge to these people so that they will understand better. More often it's better simply to ignore them.

Becoming Closer to Your Father

If your father is physically challenged, here are a few steps that you might want to try to get closer to him.

Understand and accept the physical challenge. Try to learn as much as you can about your father's disability. How did it occur? How does it affect him physically? How does it make him feel? What is he able to do? What does he like to do?

Understanding the physical challenge will help both you and your father to accept it. Your efforts to understand will reduce the emotional distance between you. Don't waste time with unproductive wishing. People are much happier when they try to make their life better, rather than wishing that it were better.

Appreciate abilities rather than disabilities. By finding out what your father can do and likes to do, you should be able to develop some common interests. You both may need to compromise a little, but you should be able to share activities together.

At the same time, you and your father will have interests of your own. This is typical in any family. It is important for you to begin to develop your own skills that you will need later as an independent adult. Always try to respect and understand interests of other family members that are different from your own.

CHAPTER 11

Sports Fanatic
Fathers

Marcie

Marcie's father is a sports nut. He has a satellite dish in the backyard to pick up all of the games. Besides the big-screen television, he has two video cassette recorders so that he can tape the games that are on while he's watching another game. Each day sports magazines and newspapers arrive in the mailbox. Marcie's father doesn't just read them; he files them and cross-references them so that every sport fact is available immediately.

When he isn't watching a game, he likes to call the local sports radio station to give them his opinion. He gets on the air fairly often to share his sports expertise. As a "regular caller," he has a special number that he can use to get on the air quicker.

Marcie's father also plays Fantasy Baseball and Fantasy Football on his computer. Using the computer modem, several people get together and choose real players for a fantasy team. The computer then compares how their chosen players did in actual games. Their statistics are combined to determine a final score in their games. This can be time-consuming. Usually on Sunday afternoons, he does a lot of channel surfing to see how each of his players is doing.

Marcie and her father have never had a close relationship. Since he has always been so interested in sports, she assumed that they had no common interests. Marcie has always respected her father. He has an important job, he was able to buy a nice house, she has many nice things. But, at fifteen years old, it makes Marcie sad that the only thing she knows about her dad is that he is a sports nut, and the only thing he knows about her is that she's his little girl.

Sam

Sam's father talked about sports rather secretively. He knew that Sam's mother disapproved of his gambling. Even around Sam he avoided the subject; he didn't want to start up the same arguments that he and his ex-wife had had before the divorce. Besides, he was behind in his child-support payments, and if Sam's mother knew that he was still gambling, she would have him right back in court.

Sam understood what was happening better than his father gave him credit for. He never asked his father about his gambling. He never asked why his father sometimes was ecstatic when his basketball team won and other times just as happy when they lost. Sam could always tell when his father had lost a bundle. At the end of the game his father would get up slowly and shut off the television. In a hushed voice he would tell Sam, "It's time for you to go back to your mother's." The ride home would be silent as a tomb.

When Sam got home his mother would ask: "What did you do?" "Not much." "Did your dad give you the child-support check?" "No." "Is he still gambling?" "I never saw him gamble." She would turn her back on Sam and go into another room. After a while he would hear her threatening to take his father back to court. This time she would make sure that he was in jail, where he couldn't bet on any football games.

The last time that Sam went to visit, his father seemed noticeably jumpy. When they drove out for a hamburger, he looked over his shoulder several times. When a nearby car backfired, he pulled Sam down and ducked at the same time. Before he dropped Sam off at his mother's, he said, "I am going to be out of town for a while. I'm not sure when I'll be back."

That was eight weeks ago. Sam still is waiting to hear from his father.

Pat

Pat's father likes to watch sports on TV—any sport! He watches baseball in the summer; football (college and professional) in the fall; and basketball and hockey in the winter and spring. He'll watch golf, tennis, or anything else if it's the only thing on. When Pat's father is home, the TV is always on and it's usually tuned to the all-sports cable channel. His idea of a perfect evening is to set himself up with bags of chips, a six-pack of beer, and the remote control.

Often Pat sits down with him to watch the games; he is a decent athlete himself and has a pretty good knowledge of sports. But each time things go about the same. At first they joke and kid about the game and the players. After a while (and a few beers) Pat's father becomes louder and more argumentative. Before the end of the game Pat usually makes some excuse and leaves. Sometimes he doesn't need an excuse: He simply walks out while his father snores on the recliner.

One Sunday afternoon Pat's friend Matt came over. They were going to hang out, maybe play a few video games. Matt commented to Pat, "Your dad sits in front of the TV all day, just like my dad used to."

Pat gave Matt a puzzled look, "What do you mean 'like your dad used to'?"

"My mom finally got tired of watching him spend all his time drinking beer and watching sports on TV. She told him that he was an alcoholic and that she wanted him out of the house until he got his act together."

"What happened?"

"He was gone a while. The first month he stayed with a friend and went to sports bars at night. He took me to a couple of them. One was pretty cool. It had five basketball or football games going on at the same time. Anyway, after a month he decided that he really was drinking too much. He went into the hospital for about six weeks to 'dry out'.

"He's been back home for about six months, now. He's real different to be around. He's more serious than he used to be, but he's a lot easier to talk to. He still likes to watch sports some of the time, but now that he doesn't drink, it's easier to watch a game with him."

For the first time Pat realized what a serious problem his father had. But he had no idea what to do to get help for him.

SPORTS IN OUR SOCIETY

Our society is obsessed with sports. Billions of dollars are spent each year on tickets, television advertising, and electronic equipment to see and hear sporting events. Sports paraphernalia—T-shirts, jackets, hats, banners, flags—are huge profitmakers for sports teams. Baseball, basketball, hockey, football, tennis, golf, soccer, volleyball, and many other sports are part of growing up for children in our society and a major preoccupation for adults.

Sports fans often identify with their favorite teams. Besides spending time and money to show their allegiance, sport fans often allow their moods and temperaments to be affected by their favorite team's winning or losing. One study showed that rates of homicide and suicide increased in cities immediately following a loss in a championship game. It is no wonder that sports have the power to divide families and distance children from their fathers.

Not that sports are harmful in and of themselves. Sports programs can help children and teenagers to develop fitness. Participation in a well-structured athletic program can dramatically improve physical fitness. Emotionally and psychologically, sports can provide lifelong recreation opportunities when the time dedicated to them is kept in perspective.

Sports can teach teamwork. Reliance on others to accomplish a goal is an important lesson to learn in life. It is important, however, that that lesson not be overshadowed by unhealthy messages such as that of the late Vince Lombardi: "Winning isn't the most important thing. It's the ONLY thing." Teamwork and cooperation outside of sports generally allow everyone to benefit or "win."

Sports can help develop leadership for some participants. Obviously not every player can be the quarterback of a football team. While some players will influence others, most learn how to coordinate, cooperate, and follow the play. These are all important life lessons that young people can learn from athletic participation.

SPORTS FANATICISM

The three scenarios above illustrate unhealthy relationships between fathers and their teenage children. Each relationship has been damaged to some extent by the father's preoccupation with sports.

Marcie's father loved sports to the point of obsession. The time he spent on sports was far beyond what a healthy person usually dedicates to recreational pursuits. He was taking time away from being Marcie's father.

For Marcie to improve her relationship with her father, it would be important for her to communicate her feelings to him. They need to find time to get to know each other. Marcie might pretend to be interested in sports to become closer to her father, but it would not really be helpful. She would soon resent trying to be someone different from herself. Marcie and her father need to find true common ground.

Marcie might find that common ground by asking her father questions about things that they both may have feelings and opinions about: "Whom do you like in the upcoming election?" "Where will we be going on our next vacation?" "What is your favorite movie?" "What was school like when you were in my grade?"

Each of these questions will allow her father to tell Marcie something about himself that is not related to sports. Marcie will need to listen to his answers carefully and ask follow-up questions to learn more. "Have you always voted for the same party? Did you ever work to support a candidate?" These kinds of questions will help her to know her father better. Once she begins to understand him, she will be better able to help him get to know what she thinks and feels.

SPORTS GAMBLING

Sam's father is in deep trouble with his sports gambling. It has already cost him his marriage, most of his money, and his son's respect. The scenario hints that he may either be in legal trouble or in debt to the people with whom he is gambling.

Sam's father needs to face up to the fact that he is a compulsive gambler. He needs help to break this addiction, like any other addiction. The program Gamblers Anonymous (GA) uses the support of reformed gamblers to help break the addiction. If Sam's father has been gambling illegally, which is true in the vast majority of cases, he also probably needs help to straighten out his financial situation.

At this point Sam can do little to help his father. Earlier, he, his mother, and other people whom his father respects might have been able to confront him about his gambling. At this point, however, Sam's best way to cope is to wait for his father to reach the point where he recognizes that he has a serious problem and seeks help for it.

SPORTS AND ALCOHOLISM

Pat and his father really haven't recognized that a problem exists. Pat had an inkling that things weren't right, but he had no idea of the seriousness until he talked to his friend Matt. Pat knew that he and his father weren't particularly close, but he couldn't put his finger on the reasons.

If Pat wants to help his father, a first important step is to talk to his mother about his feelings. If she agrees that alcohol has become a problem, they need to confront Pat's father in a supportive way. They need to let him know how much they care about him and want to be with him, and that his drinking is interfering with their family relationship. It may be helpful for them to talk to an alcoholism counselor before confronting Pat's father.

If Pat's father is *not* an alcoholic, this warm supportive approach may help him to recognize that he needs to cut back or eliminate alcohol. If he has crossed that imaginary line into alcoholism, he will need more than just the support and encouragement of his family. He will need the help of professionals trained in the treatment of alcoholism.

One sign of a serious problem is the degree to which Pat's father resists help. If he agrees with a minimum of hesitation that he needs to eliminate alcohol, the chances are that he is not an alcoholic and will be able to get control over his drinking with little difficulty. If he resists, or if he makes promises but simply continues to drink, it will be much harder for him to change.

If Pat's father resists change, Pat can cope best by talking to people who understand alcoholism such as his school counselor, social worker, a trusted teacher, clergy-person, or other helping person. He may decide to join Alateen, an organization for the children of alcoholics. The best first way for Pat to cope is to recognize that his father's drinking is his father's problem, not his own.

CHAPTER 12

Divorced Fathers

Vince

To Vince, going to Dad's house on the weekend and staying with Mom during the week seemed pretty normal. That's how they had been doing things since Vince was three years old. Vince's parents have lived only fifteen miles apart ever since their divorce. Vince has his own room at his dad's condo and shares a room with his stepbrother during the week. Vince never thought too much about how he felt about the arrangement. It just was how things were.

Since starting high school Vince has had more time conflicts during the weekend. His father's business has taken an upward turn, making him unavailable some of the time. Vince's dad tries to make up the time by inviting him to go out to dinner during the week, but both have very busy schedules.

Vince has a full and active life at his mother's house. He has friends, sports, and a part-time job. All of these are very difficult to keep up with at his dad's condo. None of his friends live around there. School and work are both much closer to his mother's house.

Lately Vince feels that he and his dad are not as close as they used to be. He only goes over there because he "needs to," not because he "wants to." Vince can't tell if the change is more in him or in his father, but he knows that his interests and feelings have changed considerably during the past few years.

Sometimes Vince thinks that his father schedules time with him as if he were an obligation, like going to the dentist or getting the oil changed in the car. Vince realizes that his father's life and career are changing all the time and that there have been more demands on his time lately. Nevertheless he is sure that he and his father are drifting apart emotionally.

Caitlin

Caitlin hoped that the fighting would finally stop. Two years ago, when her parents divorced, Caitlin was told by the court that her mother would have custody but that she would visit her father every other weekend. She wasn't very happy about the arrangement, but then she was not in favor of the divorce in the first place. Caitlin wanted her family to stay together. She was very angry with both of her parents for breaking up.

For the first few months after the divorce, Caitlin kept her feelings to herself. She spent a lot of time in her room listening to music and watching TV. She and her mother didn't argue much at first, mainly because her mother way trying to get her own life together. No one pushed Caitlin to do any chores or to help out around the house.

Weekends with her father were great. They went to nice restaurants, went to the movies, and did things that

Caitlin enjoyed. Because they had only two weekends a month together, Dad set aside the entire time to be with Caitlin.

As time passed, Caitlin's mom realized that she couldn't do all the cooking, cleaning, shopping, and yardwork herself. She set up a schedule and told Caitlin that she was expected to do her part. Caitlin tried at first, but nothing was ever done right. Either Caitlin wasn't sure how her mother wanted it done, or she thought that her mother was being too fussy.

During the year before the divorce, Caitlin's grades had started to fall off. Her parents didn't bother her about grades too much, because they knew that she was going through a difficult period. Now, however, Caitlin's mother wanted her to bring her grades up.

For the past year Caitlin and her mother had fought about grades, chores, boys, going out and staying in. The only peaceful times were the weekends with her father. He listened to her, he understood, he didn't yell at her or lecture her.

A month ago Caitlin told her mother that she hated living with her and was going to move out and live with her father.

When the weekend finally came, she went to her father's house and told him all about it. She was shocked to hear his response, "Caitlin, I'm not sure that that would be such a good idea. I spend as much time as I can with you now. I travel quite a bit during the week and am seldom home. If you were with me all of the time, we would have the same problems you're having with your mother over privileges and grades."

Caitlin felt cheated. She had never realized that she and her father got along so well because he wasn't even trying to be a parent. He was only trying to be her pal.

Charlie

Charlie's parents' divorce was ugly and messy. Charlie and his two sisters were brought into court several times. Charlie never understood much of what was going on, but most of what he heard was very critical of his mother. Charlie's father accused her of having affairs with other men, using drugs, and selling his property. In the end, Charlie's father won custody of the three children. They could visit their mother only under the supervision of the court and only one day per month.

Charlie's father seemed quite pleased with the decision. Charlie was not. He loved his mother, even though he knew that she had made some mistakes. Charlie couldn't understand how his father could be happy taking their mother away from them.

Charlie's father was a powerful and controlling man. He believed that Charlie and his sisters needed strong discipline and that he was just the one to give it to them. Each of the children had responsibilities around the house. If those responsibilities were not completed immediately, swift and severe punishment was handed out. Seldom did Charlie or the girls fail to do their chores.

Charlie's father did not believe in wasted time. Studying, chores, and athletics filled his time. Charlie was not a very strong athlete. Therefore his father enrolled him in sports camps, athletic conditioning, and strength training. Charlie was afraid to tell his father that he just wanted to have some time to himself. For that matter, Charlie was afraid to talk to his father at all.

COPING WITH DIVORCE

Divorce does not necessarily create emotional distance between fathers and their children, but it can be a barrier to maintaining a close relationship. Usually the court order is for children to live primarily with their mother. This can make it difficult to stay or become close to one's father.

Even with joint custody, it can be difficult for teens to talk to their father on a regular basis. Living in two homes with separate expectations and rules can cause conflict. In the first scenario, Vince and his father seem to be simply drifting apart. Fathers and sons often do this when living together, but it happens even more easily after a divorce. Neither Vince nor his father are having a conflict at this time. Both are busy and happy, but their relationship is slipping away.

If you feel that your relationship with your father is drifting apart, talk to him about it. Even if you are both busy, you may want to plan a weekend or summer trip together. It is possible to make up for some of the lost time if both of you really want to try. The first step to becoming closer is to communicate with your father. Simply by telling him that you feel you are drifting apart emotionally and would like to feel closer, you are making a good start.

Your Parents' Conflict Is Not Your Conflict

Sometimes in a shared custody arrangement parents use the children as go-betweens to tell each other what is happening in their lives, to plan for upcoming events, and to send messages. Often when returning from the "other home," children are grilled for information about the other parent. Sometimes the children are caught in the middle between two hostile parents. It is hard to win in a situation like this.

It may be difficult, but the best solution is to refuse to be the go-between. Tell each parent that he and she need to talk to the other directly. Let them resolve conflicts themselves.

Love and Limits

A parent's job is to give children both love and limits. In the second scenario, Caitlin's father gave her love and understanding but never set limits for her, never made any demands on her. In the end Caitlin felt cheated because her father wasn't really being a parent.

Following a divorce, some teens feel that their father is really "cool" because he never fights with them the way their mother does. This makes them resent their mother's demands even more. These teens don't realize that it's their father's failure to set limits that is contributing to their conflicts with their mother. Fathers who overindulge their children are not helping them to mature.

On the other hand, Charlie's father is giving him limits without the care and understanding that he needs. Limits and rules without discussion and compromise often lead to rebellion. Teenagers feel that if rules are grossly unfair or impossible to follow, they might as well be ignored.

Overcontrolled teens fail to develop the skills needed to stand up for themselves in later life. As adults they become dependent on others to make decisions for them. Discipline always needs to be focused on developing independence. Sometimes parents forget that the main goal in raising children is to give them the skills to live on their own eventually.

Parents Are Different

Following a divorce, it is easy to focus on the differences between your parents. It is often these differences that made them break up in the first place. People can be different without being wrong. People are often strongly attracted to other people who are dramatically different from themselves. These differences may make for an exciting romance, but they often make it impossible to spend a lifetime together.

Sometimes it is easier to cope after a divorce if you try to appreciate both of your parents for who they are in their own way. Understanding who they are and what they believe may help you to understand yourself and your own values a little better.

Divorce Is Painful

One of the prime reasons that teens feel distant from their fathers after a divorce is that the process is painful for everyone involved. People do not marry and start to raise a family with the intention of divorcing. Parents feel that they have failed themselves, each other, and their children after a divorce.

It is often hard for fathers to express their feelings following a divorce. Many men feel that they need to be strong and to maintain control. They do not feel comfortable sharing their fears and weaknesses. Many teens feel that their father is pulling away from them when the problem really is that he doesn't know how to tell them what he feels.

When both father and child keep sadness, loneliness, frustration, and fear inside, they will be less close emotionally. It is important for someone to take the first step and communicate feelings. Sometimes an outside person such as a social worker, counselor, clergyperson, or other helping person can help you to clarify your confused thoughts and feelings. When you better understand what is happening to you, you will able to communicate more effectively with your father.

CHAPTER ◇ 13

Stepfathers

The Blended Butler Family

Andrea Morgan and Frank Butler both felt they were being given a second chance to start a family. Each of them had been married and divorced. Andrea had three children: Jason, fifteen; Holly, thirteen; and Brian, eight. The children lived with her most of the time, although they visited their father every few weekends. Frank's two children lived with him about half of the time. Veronica was twelve, and her brother Ryan was ten.

Andrea and her husband had divorced five years ago. All of them went through a difficult time. About a year ago Andrea started going out with Frank Butler, and Andrea was happier than any of them could remember. At the same time, the three siblings were getting used to their lives. Holly and Brian liked Frank. They hoped that their mother would marry him some day. Jason was less enthusiastic, but it seemed to Andrea that he was going through a phase when he didn't like any adults.

Frank's divorce occurred three years ago. He insisted on equal custody of the two children. It took a great deal of compromise and discussion to make things work, but somehow they did. Frank sometimes joked that if he and his ex-wife had worked half as hard on their marriage as they did on their divorce, they would probably still be married. That was just a joke, however, since she had remarried last summer.

Frank and Andrea brought their children together for weekend outings on a couple of occasions. The first time they went to the zoo. All the children were unusually quiet and polite with one another. Holly and Brian got into a few disagreements during the day, but Andrea would have thought something was wrong with them if they had gotten along for six straight hours. By the end of the day all of them seemed to be genuinely trying to get to know each other. All, that is, except Jason, who stared out the car window, listening to music through his headphones.

The second outing went even better, although a contributing factor may have been Jason's absence. He insisted that he had an important school project due on Monday and needed time to work on it. His mother was torn, but she hated to discourage this rare enthusiasm for schoolwork. In the end, she let him stay home.

The third time Frank and Andrea brought everyone together, it was to tell them that they were planning to be married in the spring. They enthusiastically talked about their plan to include all of them in the wedding, and said that instead of a honeymoon, they would all be going to Orlando, Florida, during their spring break. All five children congratulated them. They had many questions about where they would live, who would share bedrooms, and things like that. In all the excitement, no one noticed when Jason went up to his room.

The wedding went off with hardly a hitch. The trip to

Florida was better than any of them had expected. When they got back, all of them moved into Frank's spacious four-bedroom house. Veronica and Holly shared a bedroom, Brian and Ryan shared another, and Jason had a room to himself. Jason, Brian, and Holly would all be going to new schools. They were disappointed to be leaving their friends, but each was determined to try to fit in at the new schools. It was after the first week back from Florida that trouble seemed to surface.

Holly was a bit of a romantic. She believed in "happily ever after" with all her heart. She wanted this new blended family to work. She wanted to be close to her stepbrother, stepsister, and stepfather. She made them all "wedding" presents with cards saying how glad she was to be part of "one big happy family." She went out of her way to be patient and kind with Veronica and Ryan. Her brother Brian grew impatient with this, telling her, "You've *never* been this nice to me. Cut out the act!"

Even Veronica and Ryan thought that Holly had gone too far when she started calling Frank "Dad" and "Daddy." Jason told her pointedly, "Holly, you already have a father and it's NOT Frank." Frank didn't know how to respond to Holly. He wanted to be close to his stepdaughter, but everything was going too fast. He was afraid that if he allowed this to continue, he would lose everyone else. Holly was hurt, confused; she felt that no one understood or appreciated what she was trying to do.

Jason was more straightforward with his feelings. He announced after one week that he hated his new school, he hated his new family, and he would go live with his real father if he could. Andrea tried to deal with him, but made no headway. So Frank went up to Jason's room.

Frank asked Jason to take off his headphones so that they could talk. Jason ignored him. Thinking that Jason was unable to hear him, Frank calmly pulled one of the earphones away. Jason angrily pushed Frank's hand away and glared at him, "Just leave me alone!"

Frank responded patiently, "Take off your headphones so we can talk."

Jason shouted, "No! You're not my real father. You can't tell me what to do!" As Jason turned his back, Frank turned and walked out of the room.

Brian appeared to be adjusting to the blended family better than his brother and sister. When he saw Frank coming out of Jason's room, he said, "Mom said to ask you for five dollars for the field trip tomorrow."

Frank looked puzzled. He thought that Andrea and he had agreed to pay for their own children's school expenses. But, not wanting to create further problems, Frank gave Brian a five-dollar bill and decided to talk to Andrea about it later.

Ryan walked into the living room, where Frank had gone to sit and think. "Dad, it's not fair that you're getting a dog. You know that if we get one I'll need to get a shot every week for my allergies."

Frank looked at him quizzically. "Who said that we're getting a dog? I'm sure I didn't say that."

Now it was Ryan's turn to become confused, "But Brian said you told him that you were getting him a golden retriever for his birthday."

Frank answered, "No, I think that Brian may be trying to stir up a little trouble."

STEPPARENTING

There is a great deal of fantasy about blended families. On one hand television situation comedies such as "The Brady Bunch" and "Step By Step" show happy, well-adjusted blended families working out all their problems in exactly thirty minutes (if you don't count commercials). On the other hand, fairy tales are full of stories about wicked stepmothers and stepsisters. Somewhere between the two lies the truth.

Stepparenting is the hardest parenting role for any adult. Stepparents deserve the rights and respect of any adult living in the home for an extended period of time. But a stepparent is not a parent. There is usually a testing period between stepchildren and their stepparent as to how they fit into each other's lives. The period may last weeks or it may last years. Learning to live with a stepfather requires hard work, compromise, and patience on the part of each family member.

Hard Work, Compromise, and Patience

A stepfather is not a replacement for a biological father. It is difficult for many teenagers to understand this. They often feel that their relationship with their own father is threatened by their mother's new husband. The hard work comes in trying to understand and appreciate the stepfather as he is. It is not easy to put aside your own ideas about a stepfather and accept him as a significant person in your mother's life and an adult living in your household.

Living with a stepfather requires compromise on both sides. You and he have become accustomed to a certain lifestyle. All that changes when your mother remarries. It is important that any changes be discussed calmly and that decisions be fair and show respect for everyone involved. When many changes occur at the same time, it is difficult to make each person feel that he is being treated fairly.

Bringing together two families requires patience. It takes time for each person to figure out where he fits in and how to get along with everyone else. All families experience this tension, but it is much more noticeable in blended families.

FEELINGS ABOUT STEPFATHERS

In the scenario above, each of Andrea Morgan's children reacted to their stepfather with a different emotion. These are some common teenager reactions.

Hurt and Disappointment

Holly tried so hard to make the new family work. She wanted everyone to live "happily ever after" right away. Because her efforts were criticized and ignored, Holly was hurt and disappointed.

Holly needs to be more patient. It will take time for the family to coalesce. Differences and conflicts don't disappear simply by being ignored. It takes communication to work out problems.

Anger

Jason is angry. He hasn't communicated to anyone exactly what he is angry about. He lashes out at anyone who confronts him. He is simply withdrawing from the family.

Jason's first step needs to be to figure out why he is so angry. His mother, father, school counselor, social worker, or friends might be able to help him to sort it out. He may be angry at his mother for remarrying, or with his father for spending so little time with him. He may be angry that their family isn't what he considers "normal."

Only when he figures out what is troubling him will he be on his way to working things out.

Manipulation

Brian seems to be stirring things up to make the people around him upset with each other. This is simply disguised hostility. Brian is hurt *and* angry at all the changes around him, but he expresses his feelings by starting fights between other people.

Brian may need help to bring his hidden feelings to the surface. Instead of coming out and expressing his unhappiness, like Jason, Brian makes the people around him unhappy. It will require some understanding and patience by the rest of the family to help Brian to face up to his true feelings.

CHAPTER 14

Adoptive Fathers

Lonnie

L onnie has always known that he was adopted. As soon as he was old enough to understand what adoption meant, his parents explained to him how they became his parents. When he was little, Lonnie thought he was better off than most kids. His parents gave him presents on his birthday, but they also celebrated his adoption day. They wanted him to know that the day that he became part of their family was a cause for festivity for all of them.

Lonnie has always appreciated the good life that his adoptive parents have given him. He has always had everything he has needed. Most important, though, he knows for certain that his adoptive parents love him very much.

When Lonnie was a sophomore in high school he took biology. Part of the course covered genetics and how physical traits are passed on from one generation to the next. Lonnie started to wonder how he got his physical traits and characteristics. What were his biological parents like? Does he take after his mother or his father? Does he have aunts, uncles, cousins, and grandparents that he doesn't even know about? What if he fell in love with a girl someday and she turned out to be his first cousin? He was becoming preoccupied with thoughts about his birth parents.

Lonnie talked to his father about his feelings and what Dad knew about his birth parents. His dad said he didn't know very much. The adoption was arranged through a private agency, which never told them much about Lonnie's biological mother or father. They had the impression that Lonnie's mother had lived in some kind of a group home before he was born. The agency said that the birth was uncomplicated and that his mother was healthy and drug-free at the time of Lonnie's birth.

Lonnie's father asked, "Why the sudden interest in your biological parents?"

Lonnie answered, "I've been thinking about them a lot lately. I think I would like to find my birth parents and get to know them. I would like to let them know how well I'm turning out."

His father smiled sadly, an "I knew this day would come, but I hoped it wouldn't" kind of smile. "I think it would be a mistake to search for your birth parents. Haven't we given you a good home? Haven't we raised you right? Aren't you turning out well *because* of the way we're raising you."

Lonnie could tell that his father was hurt, so he chose his words carefully. "I do appreciate everything that you and Mom have done for me. I just feel a need to know." Lonnie and his father became very quiet. They both sensed the need to drop the subject.

Lonnie couldn't stop thinking, however. The next day he looked in the yellow pages under "Adoption Agencies."

Lonnie found three listings. He called each one asking for information about his birth parents. Each one told him that all such information was sealed and confidential. They tried to talk him out of continuing his search.

Lonnie thought that his birth certificate might have some useful information. Finding it, he was crushed to see that it showed only his date of birth and date of adoption ten days later, his name, and tiny footprints.

Lonnie had another idea. Leaving all the papers on his parents' bed, he ran out and took a bus to the county courthouse. They must have some record of his birth.

Breathlessly, Lonnie ran up to the counter and asked the clerk if she could look up some information about a baby that was born fourteen years ago on February 3. The clerk didn't even move her head. She looked at Lonnie over the top of her glasses and said, "You're adopted, aren't you?"

Lonnie sheepishly responded, "Yes."

"Then you know I can't help you. When a mother gives up a baby for adoption, she is guaranteed privacy. Most women who give up their babies simply want to get on with their lives."

When Lonnie got home, his parents were waiting for him. His birth certificate was on the coffee table in front of them. His father asked, "What are you hoping to find out?"

Lonnie answered, "I don't know."

His mother pressed further, "You are hurting your father and me. You are making us feel that everything we have done for you has been wasted."

Lonnie looked at her with remorse, "I never wanted to hurt you. It's just that I've always wondered, and now I guess I always will."

ADOPTIVE PARENTS CHOOSE

Usually when there is an emotional distance between a father and his children, the gap is caused by something in the father's personality, beliefs, personal problems, or circumstances. Children naturally want a close relationship with their parents. Unless something interferes, parents and children tend to be close emotionally. While the focus of this book is to help teenagers cope with an emotionally distant father, its purpose is not to blame either the father or the teenager for the distance. However, understanding the source of the distance can help people to cope and even to bridge the gap.

Adoptive parents face a different kind of problem. The issue of being close becomes confused for adopted children. Although they may feel close and appreciative of their adoptive parents, they have a natural curiosity about their birth parents. It is normal for people to want to understand themselves better. It is difficult to understand yourself fully if you do not know your family background.

Lonnie's father has done everything to develop a close relationship with his adopted son. Lonnie is driving a wedge into this relationship with his pursuit of his birth parents. He is pushing his parents farther away by insisting on knowing more about his biological parents.

Lonnie's parents, on the other hand, are failing to grasp that Lonnie's search is not directed at them personally. They are oversensitive to his quest. It is understandable that they might not want to encourage Lonnie, but they need to realize that all people seek knowledge about themselves. An awareness of one's family heritage is an important part of this knowledge.

In the scenario, Lonnie conducts a short but fruitless

search for his biological parents. Let's look at some advantages and disadvantages of his search.

Advantages of Finding Your Birth Parents

- **You will learn your racial and ethnic background.** Many adopted children never know their racial and ethnic roots, in which many people take great pride.
- **You will know why your birth parents gave you up for adoption.** "Why did my parents give me away?" is a common question for adopted children. The answer, however, may be disturbing. Rightly or wrongly, many adopted children feel rejected by their birth parents. Few people handle rejection well. Although the birth parents' decision may have been the best one for them, the children sometimes have trouble understanding. Also, many adopted children were removed from their mother because of neglect, abuse, or addiction.
- **You will find out if you have a family background of serious disease.** Heart disease, cancer, diabetes, Alzheimer's, and many other diseases run in families. Finding your birth parents may help you to learn more about your susceptibility to these diseases.

Disadvantages of Finding Your Birth Parents

- **Your birth parents gave you up for adoption.** Although they may have had your best interests at heart, they willingly gave you up. By now they have adjusted to a life without you, and your finding them may be upsetting to them. Sad as it may sound, they may want to forget you rather than welcome you.

• **Your birth parents believed that they were not ready, willing, or able to be parents.** Finding them may lead you to expect them to be parents to you. This is most likely to lead to disappointment. Giving you up for adoption may have been the wisest thing that they could have done for you.

• **You will find out if you have a family background of serious disease.** Do you really want to know years ahead of time that your family has a poor health history? Many people are happier not knowing that their years may be short.

Another choice that Lonnie may make is to abandon his search for his birth parents. This, too, has advantages and disadvantages.

Advantages of *Not* Searching for Your Birth Parents

• **Your adoptive parents have raised you.** Most of your personality and the traits that you have developed were learned between birth and age five. If you were adopted shortly after birth, it was your adopted parents who handed these down to you.

• **Your adoptive parents have supported you.** They chose you. They wanted you to become part of their family.

• **Your adoptive parents are standing by you now.** Searching for your birth parents may cause an emotional distance between you. Unless they support you in your search, you may hurt your relationship with them.

Disadvantages of *Not* Searching for Your Birth Parents

- **You'll always wonder.** Although you may be satisfied that your decision is the right one, you'll live the rest of your life with questions.

Each adopted child at one time or another considers whether it is a good idea to search for his birth parents. As we have seen, there are advantages and disadvantages either way. One thing to keep in mind is that there are tremendous barriers in the way of such a search. The system is set up to provide anonymity for parents giving up their child for adoption.

Some agencies ask mothers if they would be willing to be contacted by their biological offspring someday. If your mother made such an arrangement, the adoption agency may be able to help you to find her.

CHAPTER ◇ 15

Previously Abused

Fathers

Jerry

"**W**hat's wrong with you, Jerry? Your little sister could have beat out that grounder for a base hit. Actually, I'm thinking of putting her in next game. I'll let her wear your uniform and see how long it takes for anyone to notice the difference." Jerry shrugged off the remarks. He knew this was just his father's way of motivating him to play better. His father wouldn't really replace him with his five-year-old sister.

The other kids and parents all think that Jerry Robinson's father, John, is a great coach. He works the boys hard in practice. He teaches them the fundamentals of the game. The bottom line is that his teams win. This year they are trying for their third consecutive championship. John Robinson won't let anything stand in their way.

The only criticism the other parents have of Coach Robinson is that he is awfully hard on his own kid. He rides him harder, disciplines him more often, and is much more likely to pull him out of a game than any of the other boys. The sad thing is that Jerry really is a good ball player, but lately he seems to be losing confidence.

The fact is that John Robinson has always treated Jerry the same way. He never gave him an inch of slack. John's own father worked hard all day on the loading docks and kept his kids in line when he got home. John hated and feared his father while he was growing up. But now that he's had a chance to think about it, John figures that he turned out all right. He is determined to make a man out of Jerry as well.

Rhonda and Marvin

Rhonda and Marvin had learned to watch their father's moods carefully. At church or at school functions he was calm as could be. No one would ever know that something had upset him. He would smile and carry on a pleasant conversation.

But on the ride home they could tell if one of them had done something to embarrass or humiliate him. If their father was silent and the air felt thick and tense, they knew that one of them was in trouble. Both Marvin and Rhonda prayed that their father would have a few words to say about the church service.

Once after an open house at school Marvin received a severe beating with a belt because his school project was the only one on display that got a C. Marvin tried to explain that there were many projects worse than his that weren't on display at all, but that only made his father angrier. "You won't make a fool of me by having the worst project in the class."

Rhonda felt the back of her father's hand across her face

when she confused two words in a play at church. The audience laughed sympathetically at her mistake. Rhonda's father felt as if they were laughing at him. He slapped her a second time, saying, "You're an embarrassment. Don't stand up on that stage and make me look bad ever again."

At a family reunion, Rhonda noticed that her cousin Angela had a bruised and puffy face. This wasn't the first time she had seen her this way. When no one was around, she asked Angela what happened. Making Rhonda promise not to tell, Angela said that her father had caught her talking on the phone to a boy. He ripped the phone out of her hand and smacked her with it.

Rhonda asked, "Why do men treat their kids so bad?"

Angela answered, "My mother says that's the way that our fathers were brought up. Their father hit them, and they hit us."

Barbara

Dominick Lazzari always did what was expected of him. His punctuality and efficiency made him a model mail carrier. People on his route could set their clocks by Dominick's arrival with the mail each day. No one on his route had ever reported receiving the wrong mail.

Dominick was the same at home with his wife and two children. Every day he got up at the same time, ate meals at the same time, left for work at the same time, arrived home at the same time, and went to bed at the same time. He had weekly rituals for running errands on Saturdays. The family always attended the same mass on Sundays, which was followed by a big Sunday dinner cooked by Dominick himself.

Whenever possible Dominick resisted disruptions to

the routine. Familly weddings, confirmations, and birthday celebrations had to be planned many weeks in advance so that Dominick wouldn't be able to make excuses to avoid them. He attended these functions, but he never seemed to enjoy himself.

At a recent family wedding, his daughter, Barbara, sat with her Aunt Louise, Dominick's sister. Barbara asked Aunt Louise, "Why is my father so rigid? Why does he have to do things the same way all the time? It's like he always needs to be on a schedule."

Louise answered, "Barbara, you have to understand how my brother and I grew up. If you spoke or made any sound at the dinner table, you were yelled at or hit. If you questioned our father about anything at all, he flew into a rage. He seldom hit me because I was his only daughter; Dominick always got the worst of it. He learned when he was very young to control his feelings and to keep his ideas to himself. He found that being quiet and keeping to a strict schedule was the safest way to avoid being yelled at or hit.

"Your grandfather died when you were a baby, so you never knew him. But I can tell you, when Dominick and I were little we were always afraid of him. That feeling never goes away."

REACTIONS TO ABUSE

Whether it is emotional, physical, or sexual, child abuse affects a person for the rest of life. Some people react by becoming closely guarded emotionally. Others become abusers themselves by mistreating their own children. Still others are able to find healthy role models or a therapist able to help them to avoid their parent's mistakes and to break the generational chain of abuse.

Although there is a tendency for adults to react to childhood abuse, it is possible for adult survivors of violence to overcome these reactions and become warm and loving people. To cope with a previously abused father, it is important to understand how most men react to childhood abuse. Knowing why a father behaves the way he does can help you guide him toward helping himself. Understanding your father will also help you to grow into an emotionally healthy adult.

Remember that abuse is never to be accepted or tolerated. If you or anyone you know has been sexually molested or injured either physically or psychologically by another family member, this abuse must be reported to a doctor, social worker, state child welfare agency, or the local police. Accepting and tolerating abuse simply allows the abuse to continue and worsen.

REPEATING THE ABUSE

It is a widely held belief that child abusers were abused themselves as children. To a certain extent, this is true. The majority of men convicted of physical or sexual abuse had suffered some sort of abuse themselves. However, thousands of victims of abuse go on to lead emotionally healthy lives.

People tend to raise their children the way that they were raised. If a father is warm and loving, his son is likely to be the same. If a father is emotionally distant, his son will most likely be a standoffish father as well. Abusive fathers have children who are more likely than average to abuse their own children. Most people are able to justify whatever they do. It is common to ignore serious problems in your own upbringing by thinking, "Hey, I turned out all right, didn't I?" This leads some men to discount the pain they are inflicting on their own children.

But the pattern of repeating abuse is only a tendency. People can break the tendency by recognizing it. Sometimes it is possible to break the generational chain of abuse simply by understanding it and making a firm commitment to end it.

Victims of generational abuse can often find help from other family members. Aunts, uncles, cousins, or other close relatives of the abusive father may be able to confront him about it in a caring and supportive way. They may be able to help him to break the pattern. Remember that physical injury, sexual contact, and serious psychological damage are never to be tolerated. If you or someone you know is a victim, seek help.

GUARDING EMOTIONS

A typical reaction for men who have been abused as children is to guard their emotions. They learned as children not to show weakness or vulnerability. Now as adults they have not learned to open up even with people who care about them.

Closing one's feelings may come from severe physical abuse, or it may be the result of minor emotional scarring. The reaction depends on how severe the abuse felt to the victim. Just as everyone experiences physical pain differently, emotional and psychological pain differ in each person. A severe reprimand to one child may be incapacitating, while another child may not react to it at all.

If a man has held in his emotions all his life, it is difficult for him to open up. He may fear that all his anger and frustrations will come rushing out at once. He may fear that he'll embarrass himself by crying. He may fear losing control. He simply may not know how to start opening up.

Most men who were victimized as children are reluctant to seek help in therapy. They are often unwilling to admit that they need help. They find it too dangerous to place their emotions in the hands of another person. If a man is willing to undergo therapy to help him to express his emotions freely, the chances of success are excellent. Taking that first step toward treatment usually requires a great deal of courage.

BREAKING THE PATTERN

The pattern of abuse can be broken with a caring supportive family or professional psychological help. It is even more effective if a father is able to have both. Some fathers realize that they have a problem and seek help on their own, but many others are ordered to undergo therapy by the court after abusing their children. If your father is emotionally distant because of abuse as a child but is unwilling to seek help, there are still some things you can do to help yourself.

Find someone with whom you feel safe to talk about your own feelings. It may be your mother, uncle, grandparent, school counselor, social worker, or youth minister. Any of these may help you learn how to express your feelings freely in a safe environment. It may take some hard work and a little courage on your part to become trusting enough to get started. But once you begin to trust other people with your emotions, you'll feel better immediately.

Second, you can help yourself by finding a good role model of parenting. Your mother may already be filling this role. If not, look for people who are raising their children the way you would want to be raised. Study the way they relate as a family. It may help you someday if you become a parent.

Finally, if your father was abused as a child but is trying to raise you in a different way, be patient with him. One day you and he may connect unexpectedly. Always try to stay open to the possibility that he may want to share himself with you emotionally and that you may be able to bridge the emotional distance between you.

CHAPTER 16

Alcoholic Fathers

Marco

Marco couldn't figure out why the rest of his family couldn't see what was happening right in front of their eyes. As part of the freshmen health curriculum, everyone had to take a six-week course that his classmates called "The Don't Class." The whole message was: Don't use drugs, don't drink alcohol, don't have sex, and don't smoke tobacco. It was the alcohol part that made Marco think about his father.

Marco's father had one or more drinks just about every single day. He drank heavily on special occasions such as weddings, holidays, St. Patrick's Day, and Super Bowl Sunday. Sometimes he missed work or went in late on the day after a "celebration." A few months ago he got a ticket for making an illegal left turn and driving under the influence of alcohol. Marco thought his father was lucky that his lawyer was able to beat the drunk-driving charge.

Marco talked to his older brother, Frank, about their father's drinking. Frank said, "Dad drinks. That's what all of his brothers do. That's what Grandpa did. So what! We come from a family of drinkers. Don't they all take care of their families? None of them are bums. They all have jobs and responsibilities. If they want to have a little drink after a hard day at work, that's fine with me. You should mind your own business, Marco."

Marco asked his mother if she thought Dad had a drinking problem. She looked shocked. "Your father is one of the finest men I know. He keeps food on our table. He paid for the clothes that you're wearing. He comes home to us every night. Mrs. Jordan down the street, now, her husband has a drinking problem. He stays out all night sometimes. When he gets drunk, he hits her. There's a big difference between Mr. Jordan and your father. Where are you getting these ideas?"

Marco decided he'd better forget the whole thing.

Rita

When Rita's father comes home from work, he heads straight to the liquor cabinet and pours himself glass of brandy. It is his reward to himself after working hard all day. After dinner he usually has his brandy glass nearby, refilling it as needed.

Rita would have to say that she has never seen her father drunk. He never gets boisterous and loud. He never becomes aggressive or violent. He never slurs his words or becomes difficult to understand. Actually, Rita's father is very calm and patient. He spends most evenings listening to music, watching television, or working with his stamp collection. As a family, they seldom go out or do things together, but if Rita ever wanted to talk to her father, she would know where to find him.

Lately, Rita's mother has become concerned about her husband's health. He smokes, never exercises, and has gained a few pounds. She worries about how the slightest exertion makes him breathe heavily and become red in the face. She has tried to drop subtle hints to him. By planning different meals, she's attempting to change the family's eating habits. But every time she brings up his health, her husband seems to retreat deeper into himself.

One evening Rita's father walked in and went to the liquor cabinet to pour himself a brandy. All the brandy was gone. He looked around and then asked his wife what had happened to the brandy. She told him that he was drinking too much, so she decided to get rid of it.

Rita saw her father's normally placid face become beet-red. He shouted at his wife, "Don't you *ever* do that again!" With that, he walked out the door and got into his car. He came back about a little later and placed four bottles of brandy in the liquor cabinet.

Tommy

Tommy had learned when he was little to read the signs in his father's face. A certain look in his eye meant that he was drunk and dangerous. If you were smart you avoided him completely. You made sure that you looked busy doing something that he approved of. And you *never* disagreed with him.

It took a few black eyes, bruises from a leather belt, and swollen lips for Tommy to learn these important principles. Either his mother had never learned how to avoid trouble with her husband, or she just didn't try. Often these nights ended with his Mom getting the worst beating of them all.

One time Tommy tried to protect his mother by jumping between her and his father. All that he earned for his efforts were a smack on his head from his father and his mother telling him, "Stay out of it, Tommy. This is between your father and me!"

The mornings after were always the same. Tommy's dad would say he was sorry that he hurt him; he really didn't mean anything by it. Then he would try to make up with his mother, but she would never accept his apology. She would shout, "You're nothing but a loser and a drunk. I don't know why I even stay with you."

Tommy wondered why, too.

ALCOHOLISM

For a long time people thought that alcoholics were simply people of weak character who were not able to control their desire for alcohol or who used it to escape the problems of everyday life. We have learned that this is not true. Alcoholism is a *disease*. It is a disease that is physical, mental, social, and spiritual.

Alcoholism is a *physical* disease. Among its symptoms are blackouts and memory loss. Damage to the liver and the brain are common following prolonged use. Addiction to alcohol cannot be broken simply by willing or wishing to stop drinking. An alcoholic who suddenly stops drinking often experiences severe withdrawal symptoms such as trembling, hallucinations, and even convulsions.

Children of alcoholics are more likely to become alcoholics than are children of nonalcoholics. Even when children of alcoholics are removed from their parents at birth, they are still far more likely to become alcoholics.

Alcoholism is a *mental* disease. Alcoholics spend a great deal of their mental energy finding opportunities to drink and ways to maintain their career and income so that they can continue to drink. Alcohol becomes the main goal in life.

Alcoholism is a *social* disease. Each member of an alcoholic's family is affected by the disease. Some members may suffer physical abuse; others, emotional abuse or emotional neglect. Alcoholism is loss of control of a person's use of alcohol. All family members feel a certain amount of embarrassment or guilt about the alcoholic's lack of control. Seventy percent of all parents who are alcoholics are men. Therefore children are more than twice as likely to have an alcoholic father.

Alcoholism is also a *spiritual* disease. Spirituality is having an ideal or faith as a guide in your life. For an alcoholic, alcohol becomes that spiritual center. Even though many alcoholics attend church and profess a faith in God, their actions put alcohol at the center of their lives.

DENIAL

Bacteria and viruses need a way to get into your body before they can take hold and make you sick. Alcoholism also needs a way to enter a family. The most common means of bringing alcoholism into the family is *denial*.

Alcoholics deny that they have a problem so that they can continue to drink. Women deny that their husbands are alcoholics because to admit it would be to admit doing a poor job as a wife and mother. Children deny their parents' alcoholism to shield themselves from the embarrassment and guilt they would feel if other people knew about it.

Denial also stems from unwillingness to change. Many women choose to stay with an abusive, alcoholic husband because they fear being alone with no husband, no job, and no home. For this reason nine out of ten women with alcoholic husbands try to keep the family together, rather than seeking a divorce.

CODEPENDENCY

A family living for a long time with an untreated alcoholic is a dysfunctional family. Dysfunctional families stay together because each member takes on a role that allows the family illness to continue. **Codependency** is what allows an alcoholic to avoid change.

A codependent is a family member who sets aside his or her own needs, wants, and beliefs for the sake of the alcoholic. The codependent believes that he is helping the alcoholic by lying for him, covering up for him, taking away his responsibilities, making excuses for him, and defending his drinking. Codependence goes beyond denial. Codependents encourage and support alcoholism by accepting it and refusing to confront the alcoholic.

Any family member can be a codependent. For the family disease of alcoholism to approach recovery, denial and codependency must be rooted out of each family member.

RECOVERY

If left to reach its full potential, alcoholism will kill one hundred percent of its victims. Alcoholism and other addictions are incurable. If an alcoholic can admit that he has an addiction and enters treatment or a program such as Alcoholics Anonymous, he enters a stage called **recovery**. Alcoholics continue to recover from their addiction for the rest of their lives.

Breaking through the denial and admitting a problem are essential for recovery. Children of alcoholics cannot force their parent to this stage. However, they can help their parent by stopping any codependent behavior of their own. Children of alcoholics need to admit, rather than deny, that a serious problem exists. If all family members stick together and gently confront the alcoholic parent, the road to recovery will be reached more quickly.

Finding Support

Few families are able to end denial and codependency on their own. Family counselors, alcoholism treatment centers, Al-Anon, and Alateen all can help families to cope with and confront alcoholism. If money is a problem, many alcoholism counselors can help families to deal with an alcoholic father at low or no cost. If you don't know where to start, ask your school counselor, social worker, a teacher, a clergyperson, or other helping people to point you in the right direction.

CHAPTER 17

Adult Children of

Alcoholics

Bruce

Bruce Patrick's father was a drunk. Today we might say that he suffered from the disease of alcoholism. But as far as Bruce was concerned, he had grown up with the man, and the man was a drunk. Not only was his father never there when Bruce needed him, but when he was there he embarrassed Bruce with his drinking.

There were fights and arguments as Bruce grew up. On the worst nights—and there were quite a few of them—Bruce's father hit him and his mother. Bruce's mother never left his father because she wanted Bruce to grow up in a family and because she didn't know what she would do if she did leave. She had no job skills and only a high school education.

When Bruce turned twenty-two, his father was taken to the hospital. He had a number of health problems: high blood pressure and the beginnings of lung disease. But it was liver disease that was taking the most serious toll. Bruce visited the hospital a few times before his father died. He felt a little guilty that he didn't really feel sad about his father's death. As a matter of fact, the strongest emotion he felt was relief.

Bruce vowed that he would never be like his father. He never touched alcohol and shunned people who did. At twenty-five he met and began to date Cindy, a woman with whom he worked. Two years later Bruce and Cindy were married. Bruce determined to make this marriage and eventually this family work. He would give his wife everything that his mother never had, and when they had children, he would be the father that he never had.

For the next few years Bruce accepted every travel assignment, worked long hours, and sought every promotion. He was going to make more money and own a nicer home than his father had ever dreamed about. In the meantime they lived in a small apartment and squirreled away their savings. Cindy wanted to travel and go out on weekends, but Bruce assured her that there would be time for that later.

When the children were born they bought a small starter house. Bruce told Cindy, "The children are small now. We'll move up when the time comes."

Thirteen years later, Bruce, Cindy, and the children were all still living in the same little house. By now Bruce was saving for college and retirement. "Just a few more years and the kids will be in college. If we trade up to a larger house now, we'll just end up a couple of empty nesters rattling around in a big old house."

Besides, there was order and organization in this family. Bruce demanded that everything be in its proper place. Noise, mess, and clutter were unacceptable. Both of the children early learned to entertain themselves quietly in their rooms.

The children had also learned not to ask for things. If they did ask, they would hear for the millionth time about how hard their Dad had it growing up, how his father never gave him anything and never spent any time with him. Bruce spent time at home with his family, although more often than not the time was spent doing work that he had brought home or organizing, sorting, or fixing things. They never really spent time together.

The children asked their mother why their father was so careful with money and never seemed happy. Cindy tried to explain, "Your father is a wonderful man and a wonderful father. He had a hard life growing up, and that has made him cautious. You know that he loves you very much."

The older one commented, "He doesn't show it very much. Other dads play games, make things, and go out with their kids. Our father never does any of those with us."

Cindy rejected this. "Your father is sober and a good provider. He is saving money for you to go to college. Don't you ever criticize or disrespect your father."

After that the children learned to keep their feelings to themselves. They told themselves to appreciate what they had and to expect nothing more.

AN ALCOHOLIC GRANDPARENT

Alcoholism is a disease that affects the entire family. Just as the alcoholic needs to recover from his disease, each member needs to recover from its effect on the family. If a child of an alcoholic does not deal with the effects of his parent's alcoholism he himself is likely to suffer from "Adult Children of Alcoholics Syndrome."

About half of the adult children of alcoholics become alcoholics themselves. This may be heredity or the result of patterns learned while growing up. It is not uncommon to be able to trace alcoholism back several generations in a family.

Many other children of alcoholics do not drink at all, but if they marry their family may be remarkably like the one they grew up in. The codependence, denial, and family secrets may all persist even though there is no alcoholic in the family.

THE ALCOHOLIC FAMILY

Alcoholic families differ from other families in dramatic ways: They are rigid, silent, isolated, and in denial. It is not necessary for there to be an active alcoholic in the family. With or without alcohol, the family will suffer from all of these traits.

Rigidity

Sons of alcoholics often are very rigid. Growing up in a home filled with denial, embarrassment, and codependence makes them hold tightly to their beliefs. They are almost never "social drinkers." They either become alcoholics themselves or never drink. They are very black-and-white in their thinking.

In these families growth and change come very slowly. When a crisis strikes, members have extreme difficulty coping. They are likely to freeze in a crisis situation and hope that things "return to normal." Things are done the way they "always have been done."

Alcoholic families, although dysfunctional, often stay together because members have learned to accept things as they are. They simply don't consider doing things another way. This characteristic makes it hard to help them. Some family member needs to recognize that the family is not functioning in healthy ways. Someone needs to take the risk to seek change.

Silence

Alcoholic families are silent. If the alcoholic is present, the silence is usually because of embarrassment and shame. Otherwise, it is simply a pattern that they have all learned. Family members seldom communicate well with people either outside the family or within it. For the alcoholic family to change, someone needs to speak out.

Isolation

Because of their silence, the members of an alcoholic family become isolated from each other and from the world. It is common for the children to feel extreme loneliness, which can lead to many other problems. Lonely teenagers often seek gang involvement, become sexually promiscuous, experiment with drugs, consider running away, or attempt suicide.

Denial

Denial is what holds the alcoholic family together and keeps it dysfunctional. With each family member silent and isolated, no one has a good picture of how a healthy family lives. When someone has the first inkling that something is wrong or needs to be changed, denial washes that feeling away.

People deny the important family issues by saying, "He's a good father. He had a hard upbringing. He provides you with clothes, food, and a warm bed." These statements deny the rigidity, silence, and isolation in the family. Admitting problems within the family and later outside of the family are important steps in recovery. Facing the truth is painful at first, but it is needed for healing.

SUSCEPTIBILITY TO ADDICTIONS

Alcoholic families need to recover and change for many reasons. In a healthy family, members are able to share and trust each other emotionally, and each member is connected to the rest of the community. The truth is accepted comfortably, rather than denied. An alcoholic family is emotionally damaging to each member.

Children growing up in these families are far more likely to develop addictive or compulsive behaviors. Some families seem to pass on alcoholism from one generation to the next, whereas other families have a generational pattern of: alcoholic → nondrinker → alcoholic → nondrinker → alcoholic → nondrinker. Each generation is really an alcoholic family; the drinking merely skips a generation. Children of alcoholics vow not to drink; their children grow up in a rigid, isolated, silent family and turn to alcohol to escape the loneliness; their children vow never to drink and so on. The genetic and communication patterns in each generation are the same whether alcohol is present or not.

RECOVERY FOR THE ENTIRE FAMILY

Although difficult, it is possible to break down the rigidity, silence, isolation, and denial in alcoholic families. It is important to break the generational pattern. Ironically, it is easier to change a family in which one family member is actively alcoholic. It is easier to break through the denial when confronting regular and serious problems.

Once a family member decides to seek help, individual, group or family therapy may all be effective. It is best for the entire family to recover together, but sometimes one or both of the parents are not ready to change. Teenagers still can help themselves to cope, change, and prepare themselves to raise a family different from the one in which they grew up. If you are wondering where to start, talk to your mother, school counselor, social worker, or other trusted adult. Remember that the first, hardest, and most important step is to open up and share your feelings and your fears.

CHAPTER ◇ 18

Drug-Abusing Fathers

John Simpson

J ohn started work at the automobile assembly plant right after high school. He made good money from the start. Admittedly, it was hard work lifting the heavy steel parts into place, but John was accustomed to hard work.

After twelve years on the job, John had a wife and three children. They had purchased a nice home overlooking a lake. John worked overtime on a regular basis, which really helped. He and his wife Karen were both surprised how expensive it was to own a home and raise a family.

One January day John and his oldest son, Jack, were shoveling snow. John must have lifted the wet, heavy snow the wrong way, because when he came inside his back hurt. He rested, put some heat on it, and went to work the next day. But he found it extremely painful to do the regular lifting involved.

After an excruciating day, John went to see his doctor. The doctor said he needed a few days' bed rest. "It's possible that you've done serious damage to your back.

We will only be able to tell for sure after you rest it for a few days." John wanted no part of bed rest. He would still get his regular pay if he stayed home, but he would lose all the overtime that he counted on.

John asked the doctor to give him something for the pain and promised to take it easy. The doctor prescribed a medication that didn't kill the pain but did make it possible to work through it. After two weeks, John asked the doctor for a new prescription. "Two more weeks, but that's it," said the doctor.

John believed him, and he knew that without the pills he would be in agony. So he made an appointment with another doctor, who gave him a prescription for a three-week supply. Just to be safe, John went to a third doctor, who authorized two weeks of pills. John felt confident that he had a sufficient supply of drugs now.

Problems developed, however. The pain was getting worse. John needed two pills now instead of one. He was also starting to make some fairly serious mistakes at work, one of which shut down the assembly line for half a day. He also had three fender-benders in just two weeks. Whenever he was at home, he seemed to be "out of it." Jack asked his mother, "What's wrong with Dad?"

Walt

Walt Howard is easy to talk to and outgoing. He's always joking or telling a story. He's the life of any party. People who knew Walt in high school and college say that he hasn't changed a bit. Most people would think that fifteen years of marriage and two daughters would change a man, but not Walt.

In college, Walt and his friends drank regularly on weekends and smoked marijuana when they could get it. After graduation most of them gave up the marijuana but continued to drink. They were afraid that drugs might be harmful to their careers. Walt, however, had always preferred pot to alcohol. He figured that he could handle it.

Walt's wife, Anne, wanted him to stop smoking marijuana altogether, but they compromised. Walt never smoked in front of his daughters, and he always kept his stash where the girls couldn't find it.

Anne wasn't really happy about the agreement, but since she too had used drugs and alcohol in school, she thought it would be hypocritical to demand that Walt stop. She and Walt had smoked pot regularly before the girls were born. In her heart, Anne didn't think marijuana was a big deal. She just didn't want her daughters exposed to it.

Late one afternoon, as she was setting the table for dinner, the phone rang. It was Walt calling from the police station. He asked Anne to get him a lawyer. It seems that a guy he had tried to buy some marijuana from was an undercover cop.

Rick

Rick Lambert lived life in the fast lane. He saw fortunes won and lost in a day's time in the stock market. Rick was a risk-taker. When his investments worked out, he made himself and his clients a lot of money. When they didn't work out, he reminded his clients that they had been warned that the investment was a risk. Rick preferred to work with wealthy clients. They had more money to invest and were far less upset when they lost a little.

People who want quick money often want their

pleasures quickly as well. As Rick developed more and more wealthy clients, he found that many of them used cocaine. They preferred it to other drugs because it gave them a quick, intense high. Rick wasn't particularly attracted to cocaine; he was intoxicated by making money. Besides, he didn't want to jeopardize his marriage, his home, or his children's future.

Following a particularly lucrative investment, however, Rick's client wanted to celebrate. Rick suggested champagne, but his client took out a vial of white powder and somehow persuaded Rick to give it a try. Rick had to admit it was the most amazing feeling he had ever experienced. A few more good investments and a few more celebrations, and Rick was becoming a regular user.

Rick's wife noticed the change right away. Rick had more energy, more confidence, and was more outgoing. He began to take even greater risks. He told his clients, "I'm putting my own money into this investment. If I believe in it, you should, too."

Unfortunately, with the risks came losses, some of them very significant. Rick felt that he needed to work harder, and more cocaine helped him keep going. The cocaine was also making him short-tempered and irritable much of the time. When his wife asked him why he was working such long hours, he exploded at her. The reaction was completely out of character. She was afraid he might hit her. She had no idea what was happening to her husband.

The next morning she told Rick, "The boys and I are going away for a while. I don't know what's happening to you, but I hope you straighten yourself out before we get back."

DRUG ABUSE

Drug abuse consists of using legal drugs in a manner or quantity for which they were not intended. It is also any use of illegal or "controlled" substances. Drug abuse is epidemic among people of all ages. When the father of a family is abusing drugs, each family member is affected in his or her own way. One child may try to protect his father, another might angrily confront him, another might cite his father's drug use to justify using drugs himself, and another might turn his father in to the police. Just as each family member reacts uniquely to drug abuse, the abuse itself takes different forms.

Prescription Drugs

Some drug abusers use completely legal substances such as tranquilizers, sleeping pills, pain relievers, steroids, or diet pills. The problem is in using the drugs in greater than prescribed quantities or for other purposes.

Tranquilizers, sleeping pills, and pain relief medication, when taken in greater than recommended dosages, give the user a drunk or "high" feeling. They impair the judgment and greatly slow down reaction time, much the way alcohol does. People under the influence of these drugs cannot drive safely, are prone to accidents, and are not able to maintain satisfactory relationships with other people.

Steroids are drugs used to promote healing in damaged body tissue. Steroids are often abused by athletes as a means of building extra muscle mass and increasing aggressiveness. The overuse of steroids can lead to many physical problems, including cancer and heart disease. The unnatural level of aggressiveness caused by steroids does not disappear once the athletic contest is over; it alters the abuser's relationships with other people.

Diet pills often contain a type of drug called stimulants. They work by increasing the activity level of the user, who thus burns off additional calories. Overuse of diet pills can lead to long, intense periods of activity without needed rest periods. This can be very damaging to the human body, which needs times of activity balanced by periods of rest.

Illegal Drugs

Any use of illegal drugs is considered to be drug abuse. Illegal drugs are used to make a person unusually tranquil, unusually energetic, unnaturally euphoric, or experience hallucinations. Any of these effects will interfere with a father's relationship with his family. Time, emotion, and money that could have been expended on his family are being wasted on drugs.

Fathers abusing illegal drugs run serious health risks, not to mention the possibility of going to prison. A son or daughter is in a confusing situation knowing that the father is using illegal drugs. The child may think that the father needs to be stopped immediately, by whatever means necessary. On the other hand, the child may feel a need to cover up for his father from his friends, his employer, and the police. Illegal drug use nearly always creates an emotional distance between a father and his children.

Drug Addiction

Another serious aspect of drug abuse is the possibility of addiction. Like alcohol addiction, drug addiction cannot be broken by wishing or willing it to end. A drug addict needs professional help. Drug addiction is a physical illness; if allowed to run its course, it is fatal.

In a family with a drug-addicted father, all members need help. The father can obtain help at a rehabilitation center. Some addicts enter twelve-step programs similar to Alcoholics Anonymous. One well-known program is Narcotics Anonymous.

Each family member needs help first to recognize the addiction. Denial is a typical response to a parent's drug addiction. By admitting that the abuse has become an addiction, however, it is much easier to help. Each family needs to learn about the nature of addiction and to understand the role that he can play in recovery.

Codependence and Recovery

People are not cured of a drug addiction. When an addict is able to control his drug abuse, he enters a phase called recovery. Drug addicts, like alcoholics, work at recovering from their addiction for the rest of their lives.

For addiction to continue, it is necessary for family members to act as codependents. A codependent is anyone who denies that the addiction exists, covers up for the addict, makes excuses for the addict, gives or lends the addict money to buy drugs, takes responsibilities off the addict's shoulders, or allows the addict to take advantage of him emotionally, financially, or sexually.

Family members need help to learn to stop their codependent behavior if the addict is to recover. Many drug treatment centers offer counseling or group therapy for families of recovering drug addicts. Alateen is an organization that has been very helpful to teenage children of alcoholics and drug addicts.

CHAPTER 19

The Parent That You

Will Be Someday

R esearchers have shown that parents tend to raise their families in the ways that they were raised themselves. Abusive parents often were abused themselves as children. Controlling parents were controlled by their own parents, and mentally ill parents usually were raised by parents who themselves had mental problems.

These are tendencies, but they are not life sentences. Parents can break generational trends of family dysfunction by admitting that they are at risk for repeating their parents' mistakes and seeking whatever help is available to break the pattern.

THE MEN'S MOVEMENT

Over the past thirty years the "women's movement" has worked to gain equal opportunities in the workplace. Careers that in the past were open only to men are now filled by women. These advances have caused some changes in family structure. Two-income marriages and working mothers have made women less available to their children on a daily basis. Preschool, day-care, and community activities have not been able to fill this need.

A response has arisen to the women's movement, popularly known as the "men's movement." Most men would consider it to be not a reaction to the women's movement, but a move to fill the needs created by the changing roles of women. Children need parents and the emotional support provided by parents. A major thrust of the men's movement is to provide emotional support wherever it is needed.

The men's movement does not try to make men more like women. Rather, it points out that all people have an opportunity to meet and satisfy one another's emotional needs. It believes that emotional closeness is not a male or female trait, but a human need.

Our society is in a period of change. Women are learning their new roles in the workplace while men are becoming more accustomed to their roles in the home. It will take a few more years before mothers and fathers become comfortable raising families different from the ones in which they grew up.

YOUR FUTURE FAMILY

Your teenage years are a time of looking forward toward your future. Part of this process is imagining the kind of parent that you will be someday. It is easy to recognize the mistakes that our parents have made, but it is much harder to learn to avoid them ourselves.

Dysfunctional families tend to repeat themselves generation after generation unless two things happen:

Someone in the family must admit that there is a problem, and that person must seek help to overcome the problem.

You Can Learn from Your Parent's Mistakes

Parents make mistakes ranging from preoccupation with their own careers to serious physical or sexual abuse. Recognizing your parents' mistakes also means determining how serious the mistakes really are. Some teenagers can become closer to their father simply by communicating clearly that they would like to be closer. When addiction or other serious problems complicate the situation, professional help may be needed. In cases of physical or sexual abuse, the father usually needs to be removed from the home for a period of time before any healing can begin.

Hope for Your Future

You are not destined to repeat mistakes that your parents may have made. Teenagers still have an opportunity to change themselves and their future family. But just wanting change is seldom enough. Teenagers with an emotionally distant father need to admit that there is a problem and take steps to help themselves and their father.

The steps may include talking to your school counselor or social worker to sort out your own ideas. People in these professions have specialized training to assist students with problems that teenagers commonly encounter. Most counselors and social workers have wide experience and can help you find out how other teenagers have solved similar problems.

Another step that you might want to take is to join a

support group. Many are listed in the back of this book. It is important that the people in a support group have had similar experiences to yours. If one group doesn't feel comfortable, you may want to try another one that better addresses your needs. Finding a support group is like finding a friend: When you find the right one, you'll know it.

A third and more serious step is to enter individual or group therapy with a psychologist or psychiatrist. You should talk to your parents before starting therapy. Often it is best if your parents are part of the therapeutic process. If one person in the family is suffering from compulsive behavior, addiction, mental illness, or a similar problem, the entire family will need to participate in that person's recovery. Your school counselor or social worker can provide your family with the names of competent therapists in your area.

The hardest step toward an emotionally healthy future is the first step. Once you admit that you need help and begin to seek that help, it all becomes easier.

Opening Yourself to Share Emotionally

Children growing up with an emotionally distant father often have difficulty opening up to and trusting other people. A way to begin is to take small risks by sharing your thoughts, ideas, and feelings with other people. You might begin with your mother, siblings, or friends. Eventually you may want to help others in situations like your own by volunteering to work as a peer counselor, a hotline volunteer, or a group coordinator. By helping others with their emotional difficulties, you will learn to become closer emotionally to all people.

Glossary

AIDS (acquired immunodeficiency syndrome) Fatal disease of the immune system caused by a virus and transmitted by sexual activity or infected needles in intravenous drug use.

Al-Anon Support group of adults who are affected by someone else's alcohol (or other drug) use, who meet to share their feelings and help one another deal with problems.

Alateen Support group of young people who are affected by someone else's alcohol (or other drug) use, who meet to share their feelings and help one another deal with problems.

Alcoholics Anonymous (AA) Support group of chemically dependent people who meet to share their feelings and help one another stay well and not use alcohol or other drugs.

alcoholism Illness that causes people to become dependent on alcohol because of changes in the brain.

Alzheimer's disease Disease of later life characterized by loss of memory, confusion, and difficulty remaining psychologically in the present time.

betrayal Feeling that someone whom you trusted has hurt you.

bisexual Having no clear sexual preference for either gender.

blended family Combination of two families following divorce or the death of a parent.

chemical dependence Strong feeling of need for a drug that causes people to keep taking a drug even when it is harmful.

codependent Person affected by another person's dependence on alcohol or other drugs.

compulsive Happening again and again; uncontrollable need to do something repeatedly.

custody Legal guardianship of a child; usually granted to a parent following a divorce.

denial   Unwillingness to admit the truth; unwillingness to admit that there is a problem in a family.

disability   Handicap or physical challenge that makes a person unable to do certain things.

dysfunctional family   Family in which some members are not having their needs for safety, belonging, growth, or self-esteem met.

emotional abuse   Psychological damage from another person's words or actions.

enabling   Acting in ways that make it easier for a person to continue addictive behavior.

generational abuse   Emotional, physical, or sexual injury to children that is passed from parents to children to their children for several generations.

heterosexual   Having a sexual preference for the opposite gender.

HIV (human immunodeficiency virus)   The virus that is believed to cause AIDS.

homosexual   Having a sexual preference for members of the same gender.

joint custody   Legal guardianship of children shared by both parents following a divorce.

lesbian   A female homosexual.

men's movement   Social movement designed to counterbalance the changes in families and in the workplace brought about by the women's movement.

patronize   To treat a person as if he were younger, less intelligent, or less capable than he really is.

pedophilia   Psychological disorder characterized by a sexual attraction for children.

physical abuse   Injury or damage inflicted by someone entrusted with care, such as a parent, baby-sitter, coach, or teacher.

role model   Person suitable for a young person to emulate.

self-esteem   Pride in oneself; feeling of being worthwhile and capable.

sexual abuse   Any sexual activity between an adult and a minor, including unwanted touching, touching of private areas, sexual comments, exposure to pornography, or sexual intercourse.

stepparent   Person married to your parent following a divorce or the death of your other parent.

substance abuse   Use of illegal drugs or of prescription drugs in a way not intended.

Appendix

RESOURCES

Support Groups

Adult Children of Alcoholics
PO Box 3216
2522 West Sepulveda Boulevard
Torrance, CA 90505
(213)534-1815

Al-Anon Family Group Headquarters (includes Alateen)
PO Box 862, Midtown Station
New York, NY 10018-0862

Alcoholics Anonymous (AA)
PO Box 459, Grand Central Station
New York, NY 10163-1100
(212)686-1100

Child Welfare League of America, Inc.
67 Irving Place
New York, NY 10003
(212)254-7410

Co-Dependents Anonymous
PO Box 33577
Phoenix, AZ 85067-3577
(602)277-7991

Emotions Anonymous
International Services
PO Box 4245
St. Paul, MN 55104
(612)647-9712

Families Anonymous
PO Box 528
Van Nuys, CA 91408
(818)989-7841

Gam-Anon International Service Office, Inc.
PO Box 157
Whitestone, NY 11357
(718)352-1671

Gay and Lesbian Parents Coalition International
P.O. Box 50360
Washington, DC 20091
(202)583-8029

Incest Survivors Anonymous
PO Box 5613
Long Beach, CA 90805-0613

Narcotics Anonymous
PO Box 2562
Palos Verde, CA 90274
(213)547-5800

National Association for Children of Alcoholics
31706 Coast Highway
Laguna, CA 92677-3044
(714)499-3044

Overeaters Anonymous
General Service Office
PO Box 4350
San Pedro, CA 90731

Parental Stress Service, Inc.
154 Santa Clara Avenue
Oakland, CA 95610
(415)841-1750

Parents Anonymous
National Office
7120 Franklin Avenue
Los Angeles, CA 90046
(800)371-3501

Survivors of Incest Anonymous
PO Box 21817
Baltimore, MD 21222-6817
(301)282-3400

HOTLINES

The initials in parentheses following the names of the organ-
izations are the zip codes of the states in which that particular
telephone number is free of charge. In the case of (USA), the
call is free anywhere in the country.

AIDS Hotline (UT)	800 526-0669
AIDS Hotline Wellness Network (MI)	800 872-2437
Alcohol and Drug Abuse Center (USA)	800 352-7873
Alcoholism and Drug Addiction Treatment Center (USA)	800 382-4357
Alexander Graham Bell Association for the Deaf (USA)	800 255-4817
American Council of Blind (USA)	800 424-8666
Council Against Domestic Abuse (IA)	800 642-6689
Calcasieu Women's Shelter (LA)	800 223-8066
Central Oregon Battering and Rape Alliance (OR)	800 356-2369
Child Abuse Hotline (MS)	800 222-8000
Child Abuse and Neglect Info (NY)	800 342-7472

Child Abuse Reporting Line (OH)	800 233-5437
Child Support Hotline (NE)	800 831-4573
Council on Compulsive Gambling (USA)	800 426-2537
Crimestoppers (USA)	800 255-1301
Father Flanagan's Boys' Home (USA)	800 448-3000
Florida Missing Children Information (FL)	800 342-0821
Hope Hotline (USA)	800 282-0062
Missing Children Help Center (USA)	800 872-5437
National Center for Missing and Exploited Children (USA)	800 843-5678
National Council on Compulsive Gambling (USA)	800 522-4700
National Food Addiction Hotline (USA)	800 872-0088
National Runaway Switchboard (USA)	800 621-4000
Parental Stress Telephone Counseling Service (MA)	800 632-8188
Rap Line Runaway Assistance Program (MI)	800 292-4517
Runaway Hotline (USA except TX)	800 231-6946
Runaway Hotline (TX)	800 392-3352
Women's Referral Center (NJ)	800 322-8092
YWCA Domestic Violence Program (IA, IL, IN, WI)	800 535-1448

For Further Reading

Adams, Tom, and Armstrong, Kathryn. *When Parents Age: What Children Can Do.* New York: Berkeley Books, 1993.

Backman, Margaret. *Coping with Choosing a Therapist.* New York: Rosen Publishing Group, 1994.

Barret, Robert L., and Robinson, Bryan E. *Gay Fathers.* Lexington, MA: Lexington Books, 1990.

Cermak, Timmen. *A Primer on Adult Children of Alcoholics.* Deerfield Beach, FL: Health Communications, Inc., 1989.

Clayton, Lawrence. *Coping with a Drug-Abusing Parent.* New York: Rosen Publishing Group, 1994.

Gooden, Kimberly Wood. *Coping with Family Stress.* New York: Rosen Publishing Group, 1989.

Golant, Mitch and Susan K. *Finding Time for Fathering.* New York: Fawcett Columbine, 1992.

Goulter, Barbara, and Minninger, Joan. *The Father-Daughter Dance: Insight, Inspiration, and Understanding for Every Woman and Her Father.* New York: G.P. Putnam and Sons, 1993.

Jamiolkowski, Raymond M. *Coping in a Dysfunctional Family.* New York: Rosen Publishing Group, 1993.

Lee, John H. *At My Father's Wedding: Reclaiming Our True Masculinity.* New York: Bantam Books, 1991.

Malcolm, Andrew H. *Huddle: Fathers, Sons, and Football.* New York: Simon & Schuster, 1992.

Miller, Deborah. *Coping When a Parent Is Gay.* New York: Rosen Publishing Group, 1992.

Oberson, Samuel. *Wrestling with Love: How Men Struggle with Intimacy with Women, Children, Parents, and Each Other.* New York: Fawcett Columbine, 1992.

Vogt, Gregory, and Sirridge, Stephen. *Like Son, Like Father: Healing the Father-Son Wound in Men's Lives.* New York: Plenum, 1992.

Index